Amazing Grace

A journey of faith, family, and the grace that bridges every generation

Dana Tramba

Quill Hawk Publishing

ISBN: 978-1-965142-68-4 (Paperback)

ISBN: 978-1-965142-69-1 (Hardback)

Library of Congress Control Number: 2025923682

Book Cover by Ava Wood, Fins and Feathers Designs

Quill Hawk Publishing (Edmond, OK)

To Gracelyn Tramba ~
Who taught us that the best conversations happen between generations, whether across the Yard at Annapolis or across the table at Sunday dinner. Your story is woven through these pages because your life has been woven through our hearts.
Love, Grandma Dana and Papa Norm

Photo Credit: Marissa Wilfahrt at USNA.

Endorsements

"Dana Tramba has written something truly special—a book that bridges the gap between generations with wisdom, faith, and grace. As I read about her granddaughter Gracelyn's journey at the Naval Academy alongside Dana's own transition into retirement, I was struck by the universal truths that connect us all, regardless of age or stage of life.

This book is a gift to anyone navigating change—whether you're a young leader taking your first steps toward service, a parent watching your child grow, or someone in your golden years seeking to age with purpose and meaning. Dana's wisdom is hard-earned and beautifully shared.

I'm proud of Gracelyn's commitment to serve our nation, and I'm grateful for Dana's commitment to sharing the timeless lessons that connect all generations in God's grace."

—**General Tommy Franks** (Ret.), Former Commander, U.S. Central Command and Author of American Soldier

"Dana Tramba has written a deeply moving exploration of the powerful bond between grandmother and granddaughter. Through parallel narratives, she beautifully captures how two lives can unfold simultaneously across generations and miles. Readers will be touched by the unique perspective Tramba offers as she shares her own life experiences alongside those of her granddaughter Gracelyn, who is currently at the U.S. Naval Academy.

The timing of these intertwined stories creates something truly special—as Tramba navigates retirement and relocation to a new city, Gracelyn embarks on her journey to a military academy. Despite the physical distance, their shared emotions and experiences create a profound connection that resonates throughout the book. Tramba's gift for storytelling allows readers to feel the joys and struggles of both women as their lives unfold in parallel.

We are fortunate to have these meaningful moments between generations captured in this beautiful and heartfelt book."

—**Nancy L Williams**, CDR (Ret.) USNR USNA Blue and Gold Officer (Ret.)

"Dana Tramba's Amazing Grace is the literary equivalent of a warm embrace. Her wisdom arrives not as a sermon but as a conversation—the kind shared over steaming mugs at a familiar kitchen table. I found myself marking page after page where her observations illuminated forgotten corners of my own experience. Tramba's greatest gift may be her ability to locate the sacred within the ordinary, making spirituality accessible to readers of every background. Each chapter concludes not with platitudes but with actionable invitations that continued to make me think for days after reading. Her parallel reflections on her granddaughter's blossoming alongside her own autumn years offer a profound perspective on the seasons of life. When she writes, 'If you want to make God laugh, tell Him your plans,' I found myself both chuckling and reconsidering my own stubborn certainties. A truly essential read."

—**Shelley Malicote Stutchman**, Author of *PEEK-A-BOOB: Uncovering Breast Cancer* and Freelance News Reporter

"Dana's new work offers a gentle guidebook for navigating life's later chapters with faith, dignity, and purpose. She weaves together intimate tales from scripture and her own life, creating compelling stories that transform the foreign territory of aging into a landscape of possibility. Her storytelling gift shines through every page, revealing how grace emerges not despite life's challenges, but through them. Dana's compassionate perspective and deep understanding of the human experience make this book both a practical resource and an inspiration for all of us seeking to embrace a meaningful life journey."

—**Tanya Cox**, RN, BSN; Co-editor of *The Heartbeat* and *Between the Beats*

Contents

Introduction

Hi Friend,

As I write these words, I find myself in an unexpected season of parallel journeys. While I navigate the rhythms of retirement community life, my granddaughter, Gracelyn, discovers her new world at the Naval Academy. Though we are separated by miles and decades, we are both learning the same essential truth: God meets us exactly where we are, whether we are 18 or 80, whether we are learning to march in formation or finding our place in a dining hall full of new faces.

This book was born from a beautiful realization—leadership lessons and life wisdom do not belong to just one generation. The discipline Gracelyn practices each morning, making her rack to military precision, mirrors the intentionality I am learning as I create new routines in retirement. Her challenges with homesickness echo my struggles with leaving the familiar behind. Her growth in confidence reminds me that God is still shaping us both, just in different seasons.

For Young Readers and Future Leaders: If you are like Gracelyn and facing your own version of formation and discipline, I want you to know something important. The character you are building through these small daily choices—how you make your bed, how you handle homesickness, and your decision to push through when everything feels hard—is not just getting you through today. I am watching from seven decades of life, and I can tell you: these are the very things that will help you age with grace.

For Parents or Grandparents: If you are more like me, watching from the other side of decades of living. Those stories that you think might be tired old tales—the young people in your life need to hear them. When I share with Gracelyn how I have witnessed God's faithfulness through job losses, health scares, and all the ordinary heartbreaks of a long life, I am not just reminiscing—I am giving her a map for territory she has not yet traveled. Your wisdom is not a relic; it is a roadmap.

Each story in this book follows a simple pattern: I share parallel experiences from my retirement community life and Gracelyn's Naval Academy journey, followed by an Amazing Grace Challenge, a practical step you can take regardless of your age.

Whether you are learning to lead others or learning to lead yourself into a new season, whether you are building your future or reflecting on your legacy, may you find in these words an invitation to see God's hand in both the discipline of daily formation and the gentle art of growing older with purpose and grace.

My prayer is that you will discover what I am learning: growing in grace is not about getting older—it is about getting closer to who God created us to be. Remember that you are deeply loved not because of what you've done, but because of who God is.

His grace is sufficient for every mistake, every failure, and every shortcoming. In His eyes, you are precious, valued, and completely accepted. Together, let's age with His Amazing Grace.

With blessings and prayers for your journey,
Dana Tramba

Embracing Grace Through Life's Transitions

♥

Gracelyn at NAPS. Photo credit: Todd Tramba while visiting a mansion with the family in Rhode Island.

But he said to me, My grace is sufficient for you, for my power is made perfect in weakness. Therefore, I will boast all the more gladly about my weaknesses, so that Christ's power may rest on me. —2 Corinthians 12:9 (NIV)

The Covid pandemic awakened something deep within me, a longing I hadn't fully acknowledged until isolation forced me to name it. Our sons lived a thousand miles away in Oklahoma, and the enforced separation made every mile feel like an ocean. FaceTime calls helped, but they couldn't replace the warmth of a hug or the irreplaceable joy of watching grandchildren discover the world.

As months of isolation stretched on, my husband and I began to sense God's gentle yet persistent nudge toward significant change. We found ourselves praying about what truly mattered, and the answer became clear with startling simplicity: proximity to the people we love most. We made a decision that surprised even us—we would sell our Mesa, Arizona, home and relocate to a retirement community in Edmond, Oklahoma—trading the familiar for the unknown at an age when most people settle deeper into routine.

The practical challenges loomed large. We would trade Arizona's perpetual sunshine for Oklahoma's unpredictable weather. Swap familiar desert landscapes for rolling plains and leave behind the comfort of the familiar for the uncertainty of the unknown. Our friends thought we'd lost our minds. "At your age?" they asked, as if wisdom always meant staying put.

Yet one truth overshadowed every concern: we could bundle up against winter's chill, but we couldn't embrace our loved ones across a thousand miles. I felt God's unmistakable guidance leading us toward a place where His grace would make possible what our hearts most desired.

Our granddaughter, Gracelyn, was facing her own massive transition at the Naval Academy, leaving everything familiar behind, adapting to rigid new structures, and learning to find strength in surrendering to something bigger than herself. Both of us were discovering that sometimes grace looks like letting go of what we thought we needed to receive what we actually needed.

This major life transition taught me something profound about aging gracefully. As we journey through our later years, change doesn't just knock politely—it moves in uninvited and rearranges all the furniture. Each new limitation, every unexpected transition, every reminder that our bodies aren't what they once were presents us with a fundamental choice: we can resist these natural shifts with clenched fists and bitter hearts, or we can receive them as sacred invitations to depend more fully on God's sufficient strength.

True grace in aging has little to do with maintaining youthful appearances or clinging to past capabilities. It has everything to do with cultivating spiritual maturity and discovering deep contentment in unexpected places. Grace means learning to find joy in fully embracing the precious present God has placed in our weathered but grateful hands.

Inspired by Gracelyn's disciplined approach to her new challenges, I began what I call a Grace Journal—a simple but transformative practice of recording daily moments where His grace becomes visible, even in the most ordinary circumstances.

Some entries capture unexpected kindnesses: "Linda knocked on my door this morning with fresh muffins, somehow knowing I needed company more than breakfast." Others celebrate Oklahoma's spectacular sunsets that differ from Arizona's desert palette but are equally breathtaking. Most often, I write about spontaneous moments that justify every challenging aspect of our move: "Todd and Somer brought the grandchildren over after dinner, where they explored

Papa's office and heard stories about his miniature steam engines and work on the Mace Missile while in the Air Force. These unplanned treasures would have been impossible from Arizona."

This intentional practice has gradually transformed my perspective on both aging and change. Instead of cataloging the losses that accompany each new season—and there are always losses—I've learned to treasure the abundance God provides in unexpected ways. The Grace Journal has become tangible proof of His faithfulness, evidence that His promises aren't just theological concepts but living realities woven into everyday life.

Moving to Oklahoma meant starting over in our seventies—making new friends, learning new streets, finding new doctors. But in that leaving, we discovered something beautiful: God's grace doesn't depend on geography or circumstances. His sufficient strength travels remarkably well, adapting to new climates and communities, providing exactly what we need for each unfamiliar day.

Each morning now offers fresh opportunities to experience God's sufficient grace in practical ways. When arthritis makes simple tasks challenging, His patience flows through my husband's helping hands. When memory occasionally stumbles over new names and places, there is a gentle reassurance in knowing that who we are goes far beyond what we can recall, and it brings a quiet sense of peace.

When uncertainty about the future creeps in during quiet evening hours, His faithful presence whispers the promise: when we feel most fragile, Christ's power rests most fully within us.

The unexpected beauty of major life transitions in our later years is that they strip away our carefully constructed illusions of self-sufficiency. What transition might you be avoiding out of fear? A move that would bring you closer to family? A change in living situation that would provide better care? Letting go of responsibilities you can no longer handle well?

Life's transitions reveal what has always been true: His grace carried us through every season of the past, His strength sustains us through every present challenge, and His love remains constant through every change ahead.

His grace was enough for the uncertain young person you once were, taking first steps into marriage, parenthood, and career. His grace is sufficient for who you are today, as you navigate this season's unique challenges and unexpected gifts. And His grace will be more than adequate for whatever transitions lie ahead—the ones you can anticipate and the ones that will surprise you completely.

Major life changes in our later years aren't setbacks—they're opportunities to experience God's grace in entirely new ways. Trust Him to make His strength perfect in whatever weakness this season brings.

Amazing Grace Challenge

Start your own Grace Journal below. Each evening, write down one specific way you witnessed God's grace—a kind word, an unexpected help, a moment of peace, a small joy you might otherwise have missed. Watch how this practice transforms not just your perspective on aging, but your entire relationship with change itself.

Today I witnessed Grace when:

Welcome Home

♥

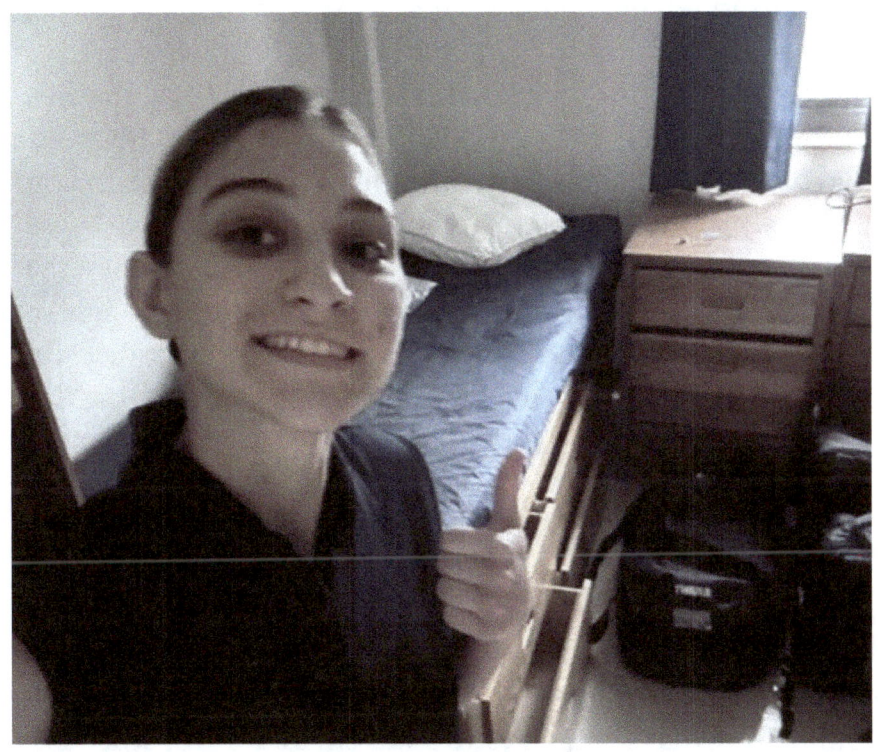

Gracelyn at Naval Academy Preparatory School (NAPS) in Newport, RI.

Cast all your anxiety on him because he cares for you. —1 Peter 5:7 (NIV)

The moving truck pulled away from our retirement community, leaving Norm and me standing in our new living room surrounded by boxes that held forty-five years of marriage. I felt simultaneously grateful and overwhelmed, excited and terrified. Had we made the right choice?

In that moment of uncertainty, Martin appeared at our door, carrying a meal and wearing the biggest smile. "Welcome home." Those two words shifted something inside me. Not "welcome to the community," or "welcome to your new place," but "welcome home."

I thought of Gracelyn arriving at the Naval Academy that same summer, walking into Bancroft Hall with her single sea bag, probably feeling equally uncertain about her choice. But I suspected that somewhere in those first overwhelming days an upperclassman or fellow plebe had offered her a similar moment of belonging—perhaps not with a meal, but with an encouraging word that reminded her she was where she belonged.

The anxiety I'd carried about this move began to ease as neighbors continued extending simple acts of welcome. Norma brought fresh-baked cookies. Harriet invited me to join her on walks. Each gesture was small, but together they wove a safety net I hadn't realized I needed.

These weren't just friendly gestures—they were expressions of grace. Grace that said "you belong here" when I wasn't sure I did. Grace that offered help before I knew how to ask for it. Grace that transformed a building into a home through the simple act of being welcomed by people who understood the courage it took to begin again.

As the weeks passed, I found myself thinking about the deeper meaning of home. The fiesta ware dishes I'd treasured weren't what made a place home—it was sharing meals with people who cared about my stories. The backyard pool I'd loved wasn't what created joy—it was the laughter and connection that happened in whatever space love was present.

Gracelyn was learning this same truth in her own way. Her dorm room at the Academy contained military-issued essentials. Yet, she was discovering that home could be found in shared purpose with roommates, in the steady rhythm of daily formations, in belonging to something larger than herself. Both of us were learning that home was less about the space and more about the sense of belonging that God provided through unexpected community.

A few months later, I can honestly say that Martin was right. This is home. Not because the cottage is perfect or because I've stopped missing aspects of our Arizona life. Because God's grace has surrounded us with people who see us, value us, and remind us daily that we belong exactly where He has placed us.

Sometimes home isn't the place we are from or even the place we've lived longest—it's the place where grace meets us in our vulnerability and says, "You are welcome here." Whether that place is a retirement community in Oklahoma or a military academy in Maryland, when God's people extend His love to us in our uncertainty, we discover that we are indeed home.

Amazing Grace Challenge

This week, be a bearer of "welcome home" to someone who might be feeling uncertain about where they belong. It might be a new neighbor, someone struggling with life changes, or even yourself if you're still adjusting to a transition. Notice how extending grace to others in their uncertainty helps you recognize the grace others have extended to you.

Today I witnessed Grace when:

Life is Like a Labyrinth

Norma Smith Garden at Touchmark in Edmond, Oklahoma. Photo Credit: Dana Tramba.

Why, you do not even know what will happen tomorrow. What is your life? You are a mist that appears for a little while and then vanishes. —James 4:14 (NIV)

It was our first day in our retirement community. I needed a break from unpacking, so I took our dog Daisy for a walk around the grounds. It felt like we were walking a labyrinth—wandering through unfamiliar paths, not knowing where they would lead or which way to turn next.

Near the raised flower beds, I met Liz. She shared that she and her husband had been the first to move to this community. "He died two days ago," she said quietly. I fought back tears even though I had never known him. In that moment, I realized this would likely be our last move, and the weight of that truth settled over me like morning fog.

Like a labyrinth, what curves and unexpected turns would we encounter in this final chapter? What joys and sorrows awaited us in these winding paths?

My thoughts drifted to Gracelyn on her first day at the Naval Academy, navigating her own labyrinth of gray stone buildings and strict schedules. Did she get lost trying to find her first class? I could imagine how the upperclassmen's shouts echoed off unfamiliar walls, how she wondered if she had made the right choice. Like my encounter with Liz, Gracelyn was probably discovering that each turn in her path brought unexpected realities. A roommate's homesick tears, an encouraging word from a classmate, the full weight of her commitment settling in.

Both of us were learning that labyrinths don't reveal their destinations. We can only take one step at a time, trusting the path even when we cannot see around the bend.

During our required two-week COVID isolation, I found myself grateful that Norm and I could walk this uncertain beginning together. We met neighbors calling friendly hellos from a distance. Dr. Leonard waved from his driveway, telling me, "Don't come close, my caretaker has COVID." Even in the community, we sometimes must walk our labyrinth paths alone; however, Norm and I never felt truly isolated.

I wondered if Gracelyn felt that same paradox in her dorm room some evenings—surrounded by fellow midshipmen yet missing the familiar sounds of home and her four dogs who used to pile on her bed. Does she lie awake wondering about the path she has chosen, just as I sometimes do? Both of us were discovering that our labyrinths require faith to trust the next step when we cannot see what lies ahead.

As isolation ended, we began meeting our neighbors properly—people who know about life because they have lived it fully. Teachers, preachers, pilots, nurses, military veterans, farmers, governors, parents, architects, doctors, pharmacists, and even a former Prisoner of War. Each person's unique journey had led them through their own labyrinth to this same center—a place of community and shared wisdom where they could focus on truly living rather than simply making a living.

Meanwhile, Gracelyn was discovering her own community of fellow travelers: midshipmen from Midwest farms and California cities, future Marines and Navy pilots who had chosen service over easier paths. She was making 'forever friends' at nineteen, bonds forged in the shared challenge. I was finding mine at eighty as connections deepened by shared seasons of reflection.

Both of us were walking our labyrinths toward different destinations—hers toward a career of service and leadership, mine toward a season of community and legacy. Each path held its challenges, rewards, and mysteries waiting to unfold. Perhaps the most beautiful discovery was this: we do not walk our labyrinths alone. God has done a remarkable job placing precisely the right fellow travelers in our paths—people who understand the courage it takes to keep walking when the way curves out of sight.

In our different labyrinths, we were both learning that the destination matters less than the journey itself. What transforms us are the people we meet along the winding paths, the courage we find in unexpected moments, and the faith that keeps us putting one foot in front of the other. Each step leads us closer not just to where we are going, but to who we are meant to become.

The labyrinth teaches us that getting lost is part of finding our way.

Amazing Grace Challenge

Take a moment today to pause and give thanks for the people God has placed in your path for this season of your labyrinth.

Today I witnessed Grace when:

Planted by Still Waters

♥

Where Still Waters Flow - Nantucket Island, MA. Photo Credit: Wikimedia Commons.

He makes me lie down in green pastures, He leads me beside quiet waters, He refreshes my soul.
—Psalm 23:2-3 (NIV)

I sat on the porch swing of our new patio, watching the morning light dance across the community garden. We had bid farewell to our Arizona home just weeks earlier, leaving behind eighteen years of desert sunshine and cherished memories. Never had we imagined ourselves living in Oklahoma, close to our sons and their families. It's said that if you want to make God laugh, tell Him your plans. The COVID pandemic had prompted us to reconsider what truly mattered—FaceTime was no longer enough. I needed hugs from my children.

Gracelyn was experiencing her own uprooting at the same time. I imagined her standing in her childhood bedroom, packing a lifetime of belongings into a single footlocker and sea bag—everything reduced to military specifications. Like us, she was leaving behind the familiar for the unknown, trading her comfortable Oklahoma home for the gray stone dormitories of Bancroft Hall.

The downsizing process had been overwhelming. Every item in our Arizona home held a story—delicate dishes from Norm's grandmother, Dad's cream separator now filled with plants. Norm's workbench, where he had repaired countless household items. I prayed daily for wisdom throughout those ten months of sorting, yet some mornings I still found myself questioning our decision.

Meanwhile, Grace was making her own difficult choices about what to keep and what to let go. Had she hesitated over childhood photos? Had she wondered if she was making the right choice as she packed away civilian clothes she might not wear for four years? I suspected she experienced her own version of my sleepless nights, questioning whether this path was truly part of God's plan.

"Good morning, neighbor!" A cheerful voice called out one morning. Soon we found ourselves gathering on neighbors' patios, sharing pie and conversation. Each person walking by with their dog would pause, visit for a while, and warmly welcome us to the community.

Grace, too, was discovering her new community—not through shared desserts, but through shared struggle. Her "neighbors" were roommates who understood homesickness. Upperclassmen who remembered their difficult first weeks, and fellow plebes learning alongside her what it meant to choose duty over comfort. While I was being welcomed with pie, she was receiving the harder gift of accountability and high standards.

As we connected with our neighbors, we discovered a common thread—we had all experienced the same doubts about our move. We all wanted to be closer to children and grandchildren. I wondered if Gracelyn found similar comfort in discovering that every midshipman, even confident-looking upper-class students, had once felt overwhelmed and uncertain.

In quiet moments, I remembered Scripture's promise: "For I know the plans I have for you," declares the Lord, "plans to prosper and not to harm you, plans to give you hope and a future." (Jeremiah 29:11 NIV) I pictured Gracelyn finding her quiet waters in early morning chapel services or stolen moments of prayer before dawn formations, learning to trust that same promise.

There was a beautiful difference in our parallel journeys. While her Naval Academy friendships would eventually scatter across the globe—some commanding ships in distant seas, others serving in foreign ports—our retirement community friends had gathered close for this golden season. As I looked over our small community garden where neighbors tended plots side by side, she looked over the Severn River, not yet knowing where the Navy would station her. But in both settings, God was preparing hearts for service. Hers for our nation, ours for this season of mentoring and wisdom-sharing.

The Lord had prepared new pastures for different seasons of our lives. By simplifying my possessions, I discovered that less truly became more. My spirit gained room to breathe. These quiet waters—the gentle sounds of bubbling fountains and neighbors' laughter—were exactly what my soul needed. Perhaps Gracelyn, too, was learning that the Academy's strict discipline created space for character to flourish in ways a comfortable life never could.

As weeks passed without packed calendars and endless to-do lists, I finally pursued my passion for writing. I read through old journals and wrote my memoir, published on my 75th birthday. Meanwhile, Grace was likely writing in her own journal, recording the challenges of Plebe Summer or the moment she truly understood what "duty, honor, country" meant. Both of us were learning that transitions create space for new dreams to take root.

While sorting through old photographs, a vital realization dawned: my life had not diminished with this move. The memories had not remained behind in our old house—they had traveled with us, just as God's presence had journeyed alongside us through every season. I suspected that Grace was discovering the same truth—that the values and love that had shaped her in Oklahoma were still with her in Annapolis, perhaps stronger now for having been tested.

Like trees replanted by still waters, we were bearing fruit in new soil. Our roots felt disturbed for a time, but God had positioned us exactly where we needed to be for this season. Gracelyn, too, was being replanted—from the soil of her childhood home to the hallowed grounds where she would develop roots deep enough to weather any storm the Navy might ask her to face.

Both transitions required faith in God's perfect timing and trust in His plan, whether we were embracing the wisdom years or answering the call to serve. In our various seasons, we have discovered that quiet waters are not always silent—sometimes they sound like new neighbors welcoming us home, fellow midshipmen encouraging us forward, or our hearts finally at peace with where God has placed us.

Amazing Grace Challenge

Take time to reflect on the values, faith, and experiences that have rooted you throughout life. What gifts do you bring to your current season and community? Remember that new purpose and meaning continue to unfold at every stage of life, precisely as God intends.

Today I witnessed Grace when:

In His Steps

♥

The Lord makes firm the steps of those who delight in him; though they may stumble, they will not fall, for the Lord upholds them with his hand. —Psalm 37:23-24 (NIV).

When I was a child in the 1950s, I woke up early one winter morning to find fresh snow blanketing our Kansas farm. The white expanse stretched endlessly, unmarked except for one clear trail—my father's footprints leading from our back door to the barn. I quickly dressed, pulled on my boots, and stepped carefully into those deep impressions, knowing they would lead me straight to him.

I found Dad in the warm barn, milking the cows while cats waited nearby. He smiled when he saw me and showed me his special trick—aiming streams of milk directly into the cats' eager mouths. That simple moment, following my father's steps through the snow to discover this small wonder, felt magical.

I imagined Gracelyn waking before dawn in Bancroft Hall, following different footprints—the countless midshipmen who had walked the same paths through the Yard before her. As she hurried through morning darkness to formation, she was learning to trust the guidance of those who had gone before, just as I had trusted my father's trail through the snow.

Years later, while sorting through old photographs in my retirement community, I discovered an image that brought tears to my eyes. It showed my son, Todd, dancing with Gracelyn—his large feet supporting her tiny ones, his hands gently holding hers, both their faces radiant with love. The picture captured something profound about guidance and trust: a little girl who didn't know the steps yet but trusted completely, placing her small feet on top of her father's shoes, gripping his hands tightly, looking up into his face, and letting love lead.

I wondered if Gracelyn remembered those dancing moments as she faced the Academy's demanding challenges. When she stood at attention during room inspections or struggled with navigation class, was she learning a different kind of dancing—placing her trust in God's guidance when her father's protective arms couldn't reach her?

This is exactly how our relationship with God works. Faith isn't about having all the theological answers or knowing what the future holds. It's about trusting completely—like putting our feet on His, holding His hands, looking to Him, and letting Him guide us through every step.

Both Gracelyn and I were learning this spiritual dance at different stages of our lives. She was discovering it in the rigorous discipline of Academy life, where each day required trusting that demanding training was shaping her for purposes she couldn't yet see. I learned it in retirement community life, where each day I trusted that this season, too, had a divine purpose.

When Gracelyn called home after a difficult week, I heard echoes of my own struggles with uncertainty. Just as I had questioned whether our move from Arizona was right, she momentarily wondered if she truly belonged at the Academy. We were both discovering the same lesson: God's love sustains us through all of life's seasons—the celebrations and sorrows, the smooth paths and rocky terrain.

I had experienced this sustaining presence through my own winters—health concerns, difficult decisions about aging, saying goodbye to dear friends too frequently. In each season, I found that placing my trust in God's guidance, like that little girl dancing on her father's feet, brought peace that my own understanding never could.

As I navigated retirement community rhythms—deciding which activities to join, building new friendships, and learning to ask for help—I was still practicing that same childlike trust. When anxiety crept in about the future, I remembered the safety

I had felt following my father's footprints through the snow, and I placed my feet more firmly in God's steps.

Gracelyn was learning her own version of this trust. When leadership challenges seemed beyond her experience, when homesickness threatened her resolve, and when quick decisions were required under pressure, she discovered that complete trust in God's guidance provided the strength she didn't know she possessed.

The Bible promises us: "The Lord makes firm the steps of those who delight in him; though they may stumble, they will not fall, for the Lord upholds them with his hand." (Psalm 37:23-24 NIV) This truth had sustained me through every season of life, and I could see it sustaining Gracelyn as she wrote her own story of following in His footsteps.

Though separated by miles and decades, we were both still that little girl dancing on her father's feet—trusting completely, holding on tightly, looking up with faith, and letting love lead us through each step of the dance.

Amazing Grace Challenge

This week, practice the art of spiritual dancing—placing your complete trust in God's guidance even when you can't see the next step. When anxiety about health, family, or the future threatens to overwhelm you, remember the child dancing on her father's feet. She doesn't worry about the music or the moves; she trusts and follows. Let that same childlike faith guide you through uncertainty.

Today I witnessed Grace when:

The Sacred Art of Pruning

Recruits in formation at Navy Boot Camp. Photo credit: Wikimedia Commons.

*Every branch that bears fruit he prunes so that it will
be even more fruitful.* —John 15:2 (NIV)

This morning, Norm and I spent time pruning roses in our raised garden bed. As I washed the dirt from my hands, I found myself thinking about our granddaughter, Gracelyn, at the Naval Academy, where she's learning her own form of pruning—cutting away habits and distractions that don't serve her greater purpose.

How remarkable that we're both in seasons of intentional pruning, though separated by decades and geography. She's learning military discipline while I'm learning the discipline of letting go. Both require the same fundamental courage: the willingness to cut away what seems comfortable to create space for growth.

As we age, life naturally begins pruning activities from our schedules. Physical limitations, energy constraints, and shifting priorities gradually thin out our commitments. Sometimes we resist this process, clinging to roles and responsibilities simply because we think we should—like those withered rose leaves that stubbornly hold onto otherwise healthy stems. But this season invites us to participate actively in our own pruning, courageously clearing away what merely clutters our days so that what remains can truly flourish.

Gracelyn and her classmates are being shaped through disciplined choices, learning to eliminate anything that doesn't serve their mission. Here in our retirement community, we face a similar challenge: honestly examining our lives and deciding what needs to be cut back. The courage required is remarkably similar, whether you're 18 or 80.

Now my gardening involves different kinds of cultivation: praying with deeper intention, sharing wisdom with younger friends, graciously receiving help from others, and leaning into our community's support. These practices nourish the soul in ways that busy activities never could, but they require me to prune away the compulsion to fill every moment with productivity.

Like flight attendants remind us: "Put on your oxygen mask first, then help others." I spent much of my life doing it backwards, often running out of energy while caring for everyone else. This season offers an opportunity to breathe deeply first, to tend my spiritual garden so that I can serve from strength rather than depletion.

As Gracelyn learns military discipline and I learn the discipline of aging gracefully, we're both discovering that true strength comes not from what we can hold onto, but from what we're willing to release. Her courage to pursue excellence by cutting away distractions inspires my courage to prune commitments that no longer serve. We're both growing, just in different gardens.

The pruning shears in my hands this morning taught me that the art of letting go is the art of making room for what matters most. Whether we're pruning rose bushes or life commitments, the principle remains the same—what we choose to cut away determines what has space to flourish.

When I look at our thriving roses, stripped of dead growth and reaching toward sunlight, I see a picture of what God desires for us. He prunes not to diminish us, but to help us bloom more fully in the areas that matter most. The cuts may feel uncomfortable in the moment, but they create space for new growth we never imagined possible.

Amazing Grace Challenge

This week, look at your commitments with the honest eye of a gardener. Choose one activity, obligation, or responsibility that drains your energy without serving your deeper purpose or bringing you joy. Practice the courage to let it go and begin

the conversation about releasing it gracefully. Notice what space
this creates in your life.

Today I witnessed Grace when:

The Gift of Undivided Attention

Norm and Dana dining with Touchmark friends. Photo Credit: Dana Tramba.

Every branch that bears fruit he prunes so that it will
be even more fruitful. —John 15:2 (NIV)

This morning in the dining room, I watched my breakfast companions navigate the familiar dance between digital connection and physical presence. Some checked weather forecasts, others reviewed calendars, and a few scrolled through family photos from distant grandchildren. I found myself doing the same—quickly responding to a text from our son before returning attention to the table.

It struck me how naturally we've all adapted to this rhythm of digital and in-person connection, each serving different purposes in our lives. Technology allows me to see Gracelyn's rare photos from the Naval Academy and stay connected with friends from Arizona. Yet something precious happens when I put the phone aside and give my full attention to the person across from me.

I thought of Gracelyn during her first weeks of Plebe Summer, living completely unplugged—no phone, no personal devices, no digital distractions. While this might seem like deprivation, she was discovering something valuable: the deep satisfaction of being fully present in each demanding moment, building relationships through shared challenge rather than shared screens.

In our retirement community, we have a different kind of privilege—the freedom to choose when to engage digitally and when to disconnect. Unlike Gracelyn, whose schedule is strictly regulated, we can decide whether to scroll through news during breakfast or engage in unhurried conversation with neighbors who have fascinating stories to share.

I've been learning to approach this choice more intentionally. When Ed begins telling the story behind the photo of his deceased wife that he always carries, I've started placing my phone face-down on the table. When someone mentions they're struggling with loneliness, I've discovered that my full attention—not a quick sympathetic text—offers the comfort they need.

This isn't about rejecting technology but about recognizing its proper place. My phone connects me with grandchildren who live far away, but it can't replace the warmth of sharing coffee with someone who understands the challenges of this life stage. Social media lets me celebrate distant friends' milestones, but it can't substitute for the neighbor who notices when I haven't been to the dining room and stops by to check on me.

Gracelyn is learning similar lessons in her structured environment. The Academy teaches midshipmen when to focus intensely on their duties and when to build camaraderie with classmates. She's discovering that authentic relationships—whether with roommates who understand her homesickness or upperclassmen who offer guidance—require the same kind of intentional presence I'm learning to cultivate at breakfast tables.

I've begun to see my daily choices about attention as a form of spiritual discipline. When I choose to really listen to someone's concern rather than mentally composing my own response, when I notice the sadness behind a neighbor's cheerful greeting, when I offer encouragement that goes deeper than a quick "like" on their social media post—these moments become opportunities to practice the presence that draws me closer to God and others.

The difference between being connected and being present became clear to me recently when our neighbor shared that she was feeling invisible in her family's busy lives. She could see their social media posts and family activities, but she rarely received personal calls or visits. Her pain reminded me that an authentic relationship requires more than digital awareness; it demands the gift of our undivided attention.

Like a gardener who knows when to tend and when to step back, I'm learning when to engage with technology and when to set it aside for something more nourishing. The goal isn't to eliminate digital connection but to ensure it serves love rather than replacing it.

Perhaps this is what Jesus meant about bearing fruit. Not just staying busy or appearing connected but cultivating the kind of authentic presence that allows real relationships to flourish. Whether we're nineteen and learning military discipline or seventy-nine and learning the discipline of aging gracefully, the invitation remains the same: to be fully present for the life God has given us, one precious moment at a time.

Amazing Grace Challenge

This week, practice intentional presence in your daily interactions. Choose one meal or conversation each day to be completely device-free. Notice how this affects the quality of your connection with others and with God.

Today I witnessed Grace when:

Together, We Can Do More

♥

Gracelyn with midshipmen squad. Photo Credit: Thorton Studios.

Two are better than one because they have a good return for their labor: If either falls down, one can help the other up. — Ecclesiastes 4:9-10 (NIV)

I joined my friend, Linda, for water aerobics at our local YMCA. After years away from swimming pools, I felt uncertain and self-conscious—would I look foolish among the regulars? Yet, as I continued to show up each morning, something remarkable happened. My body grew stronger, but more surprisingly, my spirit did too. Nourished by the deep friendship Linda and I built stroke by stroke, laugh by laugh.

The power of partnership became clear: when either of us feels like staying home, the other provides that gentle nudge we both need. This isn't just about showing up—it's about knowing I'm not walking this path alone. Looking back, I'm sure I would have abandoned this healthy practice long ago if I had tried to go it alone.

This journey of exercise woven with friendship reminds me of a profound truth: we weren't designed to navigate life in isolation. Beyond water aerobics, countless opportunities await when we open ourselves to shared experiences. I discovered this truth again when I joined a vibrant group of ladies—retirees from wonderfully diverse backgrounds, including teaching, nursing, business, and ministry—who gather each week with one beautiful purpose: to genuinely know each other more deeply. We call ourselves Women of Wonder (WOW).

We share treasured stories from decades of living, discuss current events with the wisdom of experience, and often laugh about the adventures and absurdities of growing older together. These aren't superficial coffee-chat sessions. We support each other through the loss of spouses, share stories about our grandchildren, and create a sacred space where real life—with all its messiness and beauty—can be shared without judgment.

In moments of crisis, we discover that the relationships we've carefully cultivated become our greatest source of comfort and strength. God created us for connection—both with Him and with each other. Our shared faith creates bonds that unite hearts across different backgrounds, personalities, and life experiences. We conclude each weekly gathering with heartfelt prayers for the needs within our chosen family, finding deep joy in lifting one another.

The community spirit I've found with WOW mirrors what I observe in Gracelyn, and her fellow midshipmen at the Naval Academy. Like us, they exercise together, face challenges side by side, and build unbreakable bonds through shared struggle and mutual support. They understand that individual strength multiplies when combined with collective determination. Whether helping each other through demanding physical training or studying late into the night for exams, they've learned that isolation is the enemy of progress.

Isolation is also the enemy of progress in our retirement community. Whether we are in our retirement years or beginning military service, the principle remains constant: we're stronger together than we could ever be alone.

When we notice the people God places in our path and respond with open hearts and helping hands, we become His instruments of love in tangible ways. Small acts of intentional kindness create powerful ripple effects, laying the foundation for a supportive community where everyone feels genuinely cared for and valued.

The beauty of community isn't that it eliminates life's difficulties; it's that it ensures we never face them alone.

Amazing Grace Challenge

Look around your community this week with fresh eyes. Notice someone who might be alone or seems disconnected. Take the brave step of introducing yourself and offering genuine conversation. Consider what activities you could share with others. Your interests may be exactly what someone else needs to feel more connected.

Remember: Two are better than one, and nothing is better than a community of caring hearts.

Today I witnessed Grace when:

Being a Good Neighbor

♥

A surprise celebration for an injured Touchmark neighbor, Ralph Hester, on his birthday. Photo credit: Norm Tramba.

You shall love your neighbor as yourself. —Leviticus
19:18 (NIV)

Love takes many forms, and in our retirement community,
we focus on a special kind of love—the friendship between
neighbors who become chosen family.

As we grow older, we discover that community isn't just nice
to have—it's essential. We've found something precious here:
the transformative power of being good neighbors. This shows
up in countless small acts that weave together into a safety net
of care.

When a neighbor needs a ride to her doctor's appointment,
someone steps forward to help. When arthritis makes opening
jars impossible, a neighbor appears with strong hands and a
willing heart. These aren't grand gestures; they're the daily
bread of community life.

We become students of each other's rhythms. When someone
misses their usual morning walk or doesn't show up at exercise
class, we notice. A gentle knock on the door often reveals
nothing more serious than a late night watching old movies, but
sometimes it catches something important.

I think of, Gracelyn, where she, too, is learning the vital
importance of being a good neighbor, though in her world,
they call it being a good "shipmate." She lives among more than
4,400 midshipmen who learn to trust and rely on each other
through the shared challenges of rigorous training, academic
pressure, and the vulnerability of being far from home.

Gracelyn has discovered something beautiful in
Annapolis—the Naval Academy Sponsor Program. Just as I
keep emergency contact numbers for my neighbors' adult
children tucked in my phone, sponsor families open their homes
to midshipmen who may be thousands of miles from their own
families. They create networks of care that mirror what we've

built here, proving that the chosen family can be just as strong as the biological kind.

The parallels between our communities are striking and hopeful. Gracelyn learns to notice when a fellow midshipman is struggling with homesickness or academic stress, just as we notice when a neighbor stops attending their regular bridge game or seems unusually quiet at dinner. Both communities understand a fundamental truth: survival—and more importantly, thriving—depends on people choosing to care for one another genuinely.

New residents arrive regularly at our community, each carrying a lifetime of stories we haven't heard yet. There's something magical about discovering that the quiet man down the hall lived in Alaska, or that the lady with the walker was an opera singer. Similarly, each new class of plebes arrives at the Naval Academy carrying their own stories, dreams, and fears about the future.

The magic in both places happens when we move beyond polite hellos to genuine curiosity about the remarkable lives that have led people to our doors.

What makes our communities special isn't the manicured grounds or facilities. It is the people. We're not just neighbors sharing proximity; we're a chosen family, intentionally sharing this season of our lives.

Magic happens around dinner tables. Conversations flow from current events to childhood memories, creating the sense that your presence matters and your absence would be noticed.

Every evening as I settle into my favorite chair, gratitude washes over me. The real treasure is knowing that if I don't appear for breakfast tomorrow, someone will check on me. It's having people who understand that some days are harder than others, and they show up anyway.

Every new friendship strengthens the whole fabric of our life together. When we intentionally create connections, we ensure that as we navigate the challenges of aging gracefully, none of us has to walk alone.

The true measure of any community isn't found in its amenities, but in how thoroughly it embraces every person within it. By reaching out to our neighbors, especially those who might feel overlooked, we create the most beautiful form of love: the kind that leaves no one behind.

Whether you're in a retirement community learning the art of graceful aging or at a service academy preparing for a lifetime of leadership, the principles remain the same: notice the people around you, offer what comfort you can, and remember that everyone has a story worth hearing.

Amazing Grace Challenge

This week, I challenge you to notice who might be on the margins of your community. Who needs your invitation to join you this week? And what story might you discover when you take the time to truly listen? Reach beyond your comfortable circle of established friendships. Invite someone new to join you for a meal or a short walk. Be a good neighbor.

Today I witnessed Grace when:

Precious Time

Photo Credit: Wikimedia Commons.

Commit your actions to the Lord, and your plans will succeed. —Proverbs 16:3 (NIV)

I used to fight the afternoon drowsiness that crept in during my devotions, viewing it as a spiritual failing. Now I understand it differently—even Jesus sought solitude and rest after intense days of ministry. Reading about His extraordinary work in the Gospel of Luke, Chapter 4, I marvel at how He was surrounded by crowds from morning till night, casting out demons, healing the sick, and meeting endless demands with boundless energy. Yet even Jesus sought solitude at the end of the day. I can't help but wonder: amid His intense spiritual and physical work, did He rest? Perhaps He took a much-needed nap?

As we age in our retirement community, time transforms into a precious, carefully measured treasure. The boundless energy of youth has given way to a more nuanced understanding of personal limits. I've learned that slowing down isn't a defeat—it's a wisdom-filled strategy of self-preservation and spiritual renewal. We see this reality daily as friends navigate doctor appointments, manage medications, and pace themselves through activities that once felt effortless.

My prayer life has become a beautiful reflection of this journey. There are moments when I begin to pray, only to find my thoughts drifting or my eyelids growing heavy during morning devotions or evening reflections.

Rather than fighting these natural rhythms, I've embraced a new approach. Writing my prayers has become a lifeline, anchoring my wandering mind and keeping my heart focused on communion with God. Each written word is an intentional connection, a moment of clarity amid the constant noise of life. Some days, I briefly add precious moments to my Grace Journal.

I think of Gracelyn at the Naval Academy, where time operates under completely different pressures. Midshipmen live by rigid schedules—reveille at dawn, formations, classes, meals at precise intervals, and lights out at a set hour. During Plebe Summer, their first grueling six weeks, every moment is accounted for. They're constantly interrupted by upperclassmen's commands, unexpected drills, and the demands of military precision.

The exhaustion and disorientation they experience must be overwhelming. Yet they're trained to handle these interruptions with discipline and focus. Learning to offer quick prayers between formations or during brief moments of respite. I hope they develop the stamina to "pray without ceasing" even when their schedules seem impossible.

Setting boundaries has become my unexpected form of spiritual discipline. Learning to say "no" to a social invitation, committee request, or volunteer opportunity is not about rejection but creating space for what truly matters. It's a profound act of self-love and spiritual discernment.

Each boundary I set is a declaration: my time is valuable, my energy is precious, and I choose to spend both wisely. This wisdom mirrors what midshipmen learn about mission priorities—not every task carries equal weight, and success requires knowing where to focus limited resources.

In this season of life, I'm discovering that rest is not a luxury but a necessity. Those quiet moments between activities, unexpected afternoon naps, and pauses in our busy retirement schedules are not signs of weakness but sacred moments of restoration. Just as Jesus sought solitude after intense ministry, and just as midshipmen learn the critical importance of recovery between demanding training exercises, we must honor our body's need for rest and our soul's need for renewal.

The Academy teaches that proper rest makes soldiers more effective, not less. Similarly, our willingness to embrace slower rhythms and restful moments doesn't diminish our value—it enhances our ability to be present for what matters most.

Whether it's truly listening to a friend sharing their struggles, enjoying an unhurried conversation with family, or simply being still enough to notice God's quiet presence, our measured approach to time creates space for deeper connections.

Remember that a momentary rest, a brief prayer, and a quiet pause are not interruptions to life; they are life itself. Your time is a gift. Treasure it, protect it, and live it fully with grace, intention, and love. Take a nap.

Amazing Grace Challenge

This week, start each day with the gift of presence rather than the pressure of productivity. In retirement communities, we have learned that a day's worth isn't measured by tasks completed but by moments treasured.

At the Academy, I hope the midshipmen can reflect on their schedule not as a list of obligations but as opportunities to be genuinely present with others and with God.

Pray for wisdom to spend your time well and to recognize the sacred in the ordinary.

Today I witnessed Grace when:

Don't Wrestle, Just Nestle

♥

Gracelyn and Zella loved reading and the library.
Photo Credit: Jennifer McGaugh.

Search me, God, and know my heart; test me and know my anxious thoughts. See if there is any offensive way in me and lead me in the way everlasting.
—Psalm 139:23-24 (NIV)

In our digital age, where every word can be captured and shared instantly, I've become increasingly mindful of what I write and say. The permanence of our digital footprints reminds me that our words carry weight far beyond the moment they're uttered.

Each morning begins the same way: I brew my blueberry coffee, light a candle, and ask Alexa to play instrumental hymns. As familiar melodies wash over me, I settle into my writing chair and open my heart to God. He knows exactly which harmonies will speak to my soul that day, and I've learned to trust His guidance as my words move across the page.

Corrie Ten Boom's wisdom echoes in these quiet moments: "Don't wrestle; just nestle." These words have become my compass—not just for writing, but for living. Instead of forcing my own agenda, I've found profound peace in surrendering to God's plan and letting Him direct both my words and my days.

This approach feels especially relevant as I watch our world grapple with careless communication. Political leaders, celebrities, and ordinary people discover that words spoken in haste can have lasting consequences. Social media amplifies every thoughtless comment, turning private moments into public scandals. These cautionary tales remind me daily to choose my words with intention and grace.

The passage of time has sharpened this awareness. After losing cherished family members and dear friends, I find myself pondering what legacy I'm creating. There's an African proverb that haunts me: "When an elder dies, a library burns to the ground." What stories am I preserving? What wisdom am

I passing down? My written words will outlive my physical presence—shouldn't they reflect the best of who I am?

I think about Gracelyn and the stories she's hearing in those hallowed halls. The Academy's motto, "Ex Scientia Tridens"—"From Knowledge, Sea Power"—suggests her education encompasses far more than military tactics. She's learning that naval leaders must be skilled not only in navigation and strategy but also in diplomacy and communication.

At Annapolis, Gracelyn is surrounded by professors and officers who understand that the same midshipman who learns to command a ship must also represent American values in foreign ports and make split-second decisions affecting global relations. Her mentors teach that words—whether spoken over ship-to-ship radio, in international negotiations, or during a crisis—can prevent conflicts or escalate them.

The Academy's honor code—"Midshipmen are people of integrity: We stand for that which is right"—demands that her words align with her character, both publicly and privately. This responsibility feels both weighty and sacred, just as it does for those of us in our golden years who understand that God sees not only what we write and say, but also what we think and feel in our most private moments.

The psalmist's prayer has become my own: "Search me, God, and know my heart; test me and know my anxious thoughts. See if there is any offensive way in me and lead me in the way everlasting." (Psalm 139:23-24 NIV) These verses invite God's gentle examination of every corner of my being—not to condemn, but to transform.

This responsibility to align our words with our character doesn't diminish with age—if anything, it deepens. As we journey through our later years, we have the opportunity to become living examples of wisdom earned through experience. Our words can either wound or heal, divide or unite, discourage or inspire. The choice is ours with every conversation, every written line, every thought we allow to take root. Similarly, young men and women at the Naval Academy are learning that their words and actions will either build up or tear down, create trust or sow division.

The grace that comes with aging isn't just about accepting physical limitations—it's about growing into the fullness of who God created us to be. It's about learning that true strength often looks like surrender, that real wisdom knows when to speak and when to listen. That lasting impact comes not from wrestling with life, but from nestling into the arms of the One who holds all our days.

Perhaps this is the most crucial lesson both generations can learn: whether we're in our golden years reflecting on a lifetime of words spoken, or just beginning our adult journey like the midshipmen at Annapolis, our greatest strength comes not from wrestling with circumstances we cannot control, but from nestling into God's perfect plan and letting Him guide our words, our thoughts, and our steps.

Amazing Grace Challenge

In this season of life, may we choose our words as carefully as we would choose precious gifts, knowing they will outlive us and continue speaking long after we're gone.

Remember that God knows our thoughts, which shape who we become. May our legacy be one of words that heal, encourage, and point others toward truth and hope. This week, and every week, choose your words carefully.

Today I witnessed Grace when:

Gathering Around the Table

♥

The Tramba families, making memories in Oklahoma City, around the table. Photo Credit: Troy Tramba.

*So whether you eat or drink or whatever you do, do
it all for the glory of God.* —1 Corinthians 10:31
(NIV)

In our retirement community, gathering around a table takes
on profound new meaning. It's never really about the food;
it's about the connections we forge, one conversation at a time.
Here, we learn the lost art of unhurried table talk, where stories
unfold naturally and friendships bloom over shared meals.

Miles away at the Naval Academy, my granddaughter,
Gracelyn, experiences her version of this timeless ritual. Each
day, midshipmen gather around tables in King Hall, sharing
meals that fuel not just their bodies but their brotherhood and
sisterhood. I wonder about Grace's table companions—what
stories are they sharing between the bites of Navy chow? Are
they forging the kind of bonds that will carry them through
challenges ahead?

In both our communities—one bound by a shared
experience of decades lived, the other by a shared commitment
to serving—the dining table becomes a sacred space. In a
world overwhelmed by turmoil, our communal dining rooms
become sanctuaries where we can set aside worries and focus
on what truly matters: the person sitting across from us, the
laughter echoing from nearby tables, and the gentle rhythm of
genuine conversation.

Our meals weave together into rich tapestries of connection.
In my retirement community, we chat with servers who could
be our grandchildren, their youthful energy brightening our
days. We welcome new residents with curiosity, discovering
surprising threads that connect our lives. At the Academy,
Grace and her fellow midshipmen meet new plebes,
understanding that today's stranger becomes tomorrow's
shipmate.

New acquaintances gradually become trusted friends, then evolve into members of our chosen family. I imagine Gracelyn experiencing the same transformation—classmates becoming squadmates, squadmates becoming lifelong friends who will stand by each other through deployments and challenges we can't yet imagine.

If you find yourself dining alone in your apartment, I urge you to reconsider. Step into the communal dining room and open yourself to the delightful uncertainty of new connections. Gracelyn doesn't have the luxury of eating alone; every meal is communal by design. Perhaps there's wisdom in this structure, as embracing spontaneity often leads to friendships that enrich our lives in unexpected ways.

The beauty of table fellowship extends beyond both our retirement community walls and the Academy's gates. When Gracelyn comes home on leave, we arrive to enthusiastic greetings from family and unconditional love of family dogs, whose tail-wagging welcome sets a warm tone for the entire visit.

During these family gatherings, we have learned to sit back and savor the hospitality our children provide. The greatest gift isn't the perfectly prepared meal, it's the shared laughter, gentle teasing, and stories that fill the room. Gracelyn brings tales from Annapolis—classmates, challenges overcome, traditions honored. We share stories from our community—new friendships formed, small victories celebrated, wisdom gained.

Generations have changed their approach to hospitality. Years ago, I would have set the table the night before, with every dish prepared and served at precisely the planned time. Today's generation embraces a more relaxed rhythm—grabbing plates and finding spots as food appears in waves. At the Academy, meals follow military precision, yet even within that structure, genuine moments emerge between the protocol.

However, I have discovered that neither the timing nor the formality matters. What matters is the unhurried time we spend together, the stories that emerge between courses, and the love that fills the spaces between our words. The imperfect timing becomes part of the charm, creating more authentic memories than any flawlessly orchestrated meal.

As visits end and we return to our retirement community, I carry with me deep gratitude for the time spent with loved ones. When Grace returns to Annapolis, she carries our love back to her chosen naval family. Gracelyn and her fellow midshipmen are creating their chosen family now—bonds forged in shared challenges, strengthened around shared tables. They'll scatter to ships and stations worldwide, but connections formed over countless meals will endure.

The table, it turns out, is where life happens. It's where we celebrate milestones and mourn losses, share dreams and offer comfort, laugh until our sides ache, and sometimes cry together over life's unexpected turns. Around tables—whether with biological families, Academy squadmates, or retirement community friends—we discover that we're never truly alone.

Amazing Grace Challenge

Remember this: when you gather with family in their homes, the goal is connection, not perfection. No one should dine alone, whether at home, in our retirement community, or in the structured halls of service academies. Grow your chosen family by extending invitations to those dining alone and creating connections that nourish both body and soul.

Today I witnessed Grace when:

Route 66: The Journey of a Lifetime

♥

At Route 66 Mother Road Museum in Victorville, California.
Photo credit: Norm Tramba.

Have I not commanded you? Be strong and courageous. Do not be afraid, do not be discourage, for the Lord your God will be with you wherever you go.
—Joshua 1:9 (NIV)

With bittersweet tears streaming down my cheeks, I bid farewell to my graduating classmates in the summer of 1966. Our tight-knit group of fifteen had shared twelve years in our small farm community, where everyone knew everyone and dreams seemed as vast as the endless cornfields surrounding us.

What we didn't fully appreciate at the time was that around the time of our birth, Route 66 was being established as America's legendary highway. This Mother Road would come to symbolize freedom, exploration, and the untamed spirit that beckons travelers to venture beyond the familiar. It captured the same exhilarating sense of possibility we felt as eighteen-year-olds ready to venture beyond our hometown boundaries.

Now, decades later, I watch my granddaughter Grace embark on her own version of Route 66—not the asphalt ribbon stretching from Chicago to Santa Monica, but the rigorous path through the Naval Academy that will lead her to unknown destinations. Like those early Route 66 travelers, she has chosen a route that promises adventure, challenges, and character-building experiences that come from venturing far beyond the familiar.

A decade after graduation, life introduced me to Norm, who became not just my husband but my favorite Route 66 traveling companion. We discovered our shared passion for the highway's character-filled attractions—quirky roadside oddities that make us laugh, warm hospitality of mom-and-pop diners where conversations linger over coffee refills, and timeless slices of Americana we collect like precious souvenirs.

Gracelyn is now collecting her own treasures. Not vintage postcards or neon sign photographs, but friendships forged in shared challenges, lessons learned from demanding instructors, and memories made in the hallowed halls of Bancroft Hall. Her journey requires different kinds of courage than ours did, but the essence remains the same: stepping boldly into the unknown with faith that the road ahead holds purpose.

Our Route 66 travels are never about checking destinations off a list or rushing toward endpoints. Instead, we have mastered the art of savoring the journey itself. We often yield to the spontaneous urge to explore whatever catches our eye—a vintage gas station, a mysterious historical marker, or simply a scenic overlook that promises a perfect sunset.

One vivid memory remains from our visit to the Route 66 Mother Road Museum in Victorville, California. I can still picture myself sitting in that flower-painted Volkswagen Bug, surrounded by authentic neon signs, gleaming classic cars, and carefully preserved artifacts that honored the highway's golden age. These weren't just museum pieces—they were tangible connections to American history, each telling stories of freedom and adventure. Gracelyn is forging her own connections to American history, walking the same paths as countless naval officers before her.

Fifty years after graduation, I reunited with my Class of '66. Looking back with the wisdom of decades, we marveled at how differently our lives had unfolded from those earnest teenage dreams. Back then, we harbored straightforward aspirations: to become teachers, nurses, secretaries, and mothers. Life, however, had crafted other plans entirely.

Like Route 66 itself, with its realignments and rerouting over the decades, our lives have taken unexpected turns. These experiences have taught us profound lessons about resilience and adaptability. Life's detours, however challenging or surprising, often lead to unforeseen blessings and growth we never could have imagined.

Grace's path seems more defined than ours was at eighteen—four years at the Academy, followed by a five-year service commitment. But I suspect she'll discover what we have learned: that even the most carefully mapped routes encounter unexpected detours. The Navy will send her places she has never imagined, introduce her to challenges she hasn't anticipated, and shape her in ways no curriculum could predict.

Today, Norm and I have made our home in Oklahoma, where the spirit of Route 66 remains vibrantly alive. When nostalgia calls, we make our pilgrimage to POPS in Arcadia, a delightful throwback to simpler times. This old-fashioned diner charms us with its incredible selection of over 600 varieties of sodas, each bottle promising a different adventure for our taste buds.

Gracelyn used to live here along Route 66. Now we have no idea what roads she will travel in the Navy, what ports will become her temporary homes, what challenges will test her resolve. However, I am certain she will face unexpected turns and meet people in unexpected places—just as all travelers do.

Four Star General Tommy Franks (Ret.) and his wife Cathy with Gracelyn. Photo Credit: Todd Tramba.

The night before she flew back to Annapolis, she dined with us, her parents, and our new friends—Four Star General Tommy Franks (Ret.) and his wife Cathy. What a special evening, filled with the kind of unexpected connections that make life's journey so remarkable. General Franks shared words of wisdom his father had given him, advice that applies whether you're navigating Route 66 or charting a course through life: Be FEISTY.

F - Focus
E – Energy
I - Integrity
S - Solve the problem
T - Take responsibility
Y - Say yes to opportunities

This acronym captures the spirit that Route 66 travelers have always needed—the courage to face whatever lies around the next bend with determination, honesty, and an adventurous heart. Gracelyn will need these same qualities as she navigates her naval career, just as we all need them as we continue our journeys through life.

Like the Mother Road that has taught generations of travelers to embrace the unexpected, life's greatest lesson is that the journey itself is meant to be savored and explored with curiosity and wonder. True fulfillment comes not from rigidly following predetermined destinations, but from embracing life's beautiful unpredictability and remaining open to detours that initially seem like interruptions.

Often, these unplanned side trips are similar to the career changes we never saw coming. The relationships that bloomed in unexpected places. The challenges that forced us to discover hidden strength, create our most treasured memories, and shape us into the people we were meant to become.

Grace's journey is just beginning, but she is already learning what Route 66 has taught us: that the most meaningful destinations are often the ones we never planned to visit. The most valuable souvenirs are the relationships we build and the character we develop along the way.

Amazing Grace Challenge

Take time to reflect on the roads you have traveled, both literal and metaphorical. Consider how those unexpected turns, the ones that initially caused worry or disappointment, ultimately became sources of your greatest blessings and personal growth.

Share these insights with the children and young adults in your life. Inspire them to be courageous explorers, encouraging them to step boldly into the unknown with confidence and embrace life's journey with open hearts and minds ready for adventure. Remember that sometimes the most beautiful destinations are the ones we never planned to visit.

If you are a young leader exploring the world, remember your parents and grandparents would love to hear your stories.

Today I witnessed Grace when:

Using Your Gifts –
Walking the Talk

♥

Gracelyn home for Navy vs. Tulsa University football game. Navy Won! Go Navy! Photo Credit: Todd Tramba.

In the same way, let your light shine before others, so that they may see your good works and give glory to your Father who is in heaven. —Matthew 5:16 NIV)

We all know people who are masters at "talking the talk" but fall short when it comes to "walking the talk." Their words ring hollow because actions—or the lack of them—always speak louder than words.

The difference between talking and walking becomes crystal clear in the ancient Bible story of Joseph. Here was a young man who spent more time talking about his greatness than demonstrating it. Joseph flaunted his colorful coat and boasted about dreams where his family would bow down to him. His brothers grew weary of his empty boasting and eventually threw him into a well and sold him into slavery. In one devastating moment, Joseph learned that talking about being special and living with wisdom are two very different things.

This ancient story reminds me of Gracelyn during her first weeks at the Naval Academy. Like Joseph in his well, the plebes can only look upward toward the demanding standards they must meet and the character they must develop.

Initially, I wanted to protect Gracelyn from what seems unnecessarily harsh. Then I realize something profound: they're learning to walk the talk Navy-style, being taught to speak with authority earned through action. She can no longer rely on being the bright student who talks about her potential. She must demonstrate it daily through her actions, perseverance, and willingness to serve others, even when exhausted.

This transformation reminds me of two friends who embody what "walking the talk" truly looks like in our retirement community: Nancy and Myron.

Nancy doesn't give speeches about compassion. Instead, she quietly transforms donated wedding dresses into burial clothes for babies who won't survive. Hours of careful stitching carry her prayers and tears. She rarely speaks about this ministry, but her needle and thread speak volumes about love in action.

Myron doesn't lecture others about generosity. He mends clothes for anyone who needs help, never charging a fee. While others might talk about serving the community, Myron's hands do the serving. Both Nancy and Myron have discovered that walking the talk often happens in silence, through consistent acts of love rather than grand declarations.

Joseph's transformation began at the bottom of that well, where his only view was upward toward God. Stripped of his coat and status, he could no longer rely on words alone. He learned to ask, "What should I do now?" and then actually do it.

Grace is learning this same lesson at the Academy. When exhaustion threatens to overwhelm her, she can't just talk about perseverance—she must persevere. She can't simply discuss teamwork—she must be the teammate others can count on. Everyday strips away another layer of who she thought she was, revealing who she's becoming through her choices and actions.

As we navigate the challenges of aging, we each face our version of Joseph's well or Gracelyn's Plebe Summer. We can spend our time talking about what we used to do, or we can ask the transformative question: "What should I do now?"

This is where walking the talk becomes most meaningful. Our gifts haven't expired—they have been refined by experience and seasoned with wisdom. The question isn't whether we still have something to offer, but whether we'll offer it through action rather than just conversation.

Nancy and Myron understand this. They don't spend time talking about their limitations or dwelling on what they used to do. They focus on what they can do today. Their skills, combined with willing hearts, become instruments of grace.

Each season of life presents new opportunities to align our actions with our words. Perhaps someone in our retirement community needs encouragement, and we can offer it. Perhaps there's a skill we can share or a simple act of kindness we can perform. These aren't the subjects of lengthy speeches; they're the substance of lives well-lived.

Gracelyn is learning this lesson at nineteen, under the demanding training of the Naval Academy. Nancy and Myron have discovered it through decades of quiet service. Joseph learned it through hardship and eventual triumph. The lesson remains the same: walking the talk means moving beyond good intentions to faithful actions.

Amazing Grace Challenge

This week, move beyond good intentions to faithful action. Look around your community and ask yourself: "What should I do now?"

Whether it's mending something broken, offering encouragement to someone struggling, or using a skill you've been talking about sharing—take that first step. Like Nancy with her needle, like Myron with his repairs, like Gracelyn learning to serve under pressure, discover that your most meaningful impact often happens through quiet, consistent actions rather than grand declarations.

Remember: your gifts haven't expired—they've been refined by experience. What will you do with them today?

Today I witnessed Grace when:

I Like to Walk with Papa

Papa Norm walking with Elijah in Oklahoma City. (2005)
Photo Credit: Todd Tramba.

The Lord makes firm the steps of those who delight in him; though they may stumble, they will not fall, for the Lord upholds them with his hand. —Psalm 37:23-24 (NIV)

Walking out of the YMCA, I paused as a mother hurried past, gently tugging her daughter's hand. They were clearly on a schedule—the little girl needed to be dropped off at childcare so Mom could continue her packed day. But the child, dressed in a frilly red dress and pristine white shoes, stopped despite her mother's urgency to examine the vibrant pansies lining the sidewalk.

I saw myself in that mother. How often had I rushed from one task to another, mentally checking boxes off my endless to-do list, missing the beauty surrounding me because I was too busy hurrying toward the next obligation?

The scene brought to mind a treasured memory of my husband, Norm, walking with our first grandson, Elijah, when he was about two years old. While we adults were caught up in busy schedules, Elijah would point out every ladybug, beetle, flower, and bird to his Papa. And Norm never rushed him. He paused whenever Elijah wanted to examine each tiny creature, as if that beetle were the most fascinating thing in the world.

Their patient explorations reminded me of a poem from an unknown author that had stayed with me for years:

I like to walk with Grandpa.
His steps are short, like mine.
He never says, "Now hurry up."
He always takes his time.

Most people have to hurry;
they never stop to see.

I'm so glad that God made Grandpa
unrushed and young, like me.

Meanwhile, hundreds of miles away, Gracelyn was probably hurrying across the Naval Academy Yard for formation. But her military world was teaching her something surprising: the Academy's rigid schedule didn't rush midshipmen through character development—it created space for them to be fully present in each moment that mattered.

Gracelyn had discovered unexpected moments of beauty at Annapolis—morning light hitting the chapel dome, the sound of the Navy band practicing, the quiet satisfaction of a room inspection passed with flying colors. The demanding schedule hadn't dulled her ability to notice; it had sharpened it. She was learning that presence wasn't about having unlimited time; it was about bringing complete attention to the time you had.

This realization had become clearer since Norm and I moved to our retirement community. We had come to be closer to our children, but this choice had given us something more valuable: the opportunity to slow down and truly see. Just as Gracelyn was learning presence within structure, I was discovering presence within freedom.

In our community, I had found my own version of standing watch. When I sat on our patio in early morning, coffee in hand, watching neighbors tend their garden plots, I was practicing the same mindfulness Gracelyn exercised during her quiet hours of duty. We were both learning that being truly present transformed ordinary moments into something sacred.

Yesterday, when our neighbor's great-grandson visited, I watched him examine a butterfly on the flower bed. His wonder reminded me of Elijah with his beetles, and I thought about how this same curiosity lived in Gracelyn as she spotted herons fishing in Chesapeake Bay. Three generations, learning the same lesson: beauty revealed itself to those who took time to truly see.

Looking back, I realized what I had missed during those busy parenting years. I had been so focused on getting to the next thing that I missed the thing right in front of me. But Gracelyn wouldn't make that mistake. Her military training was teaching her what it had taken me decades to learn: true excellence required both discipline and presence.

The Bible promises us: "The Lord makes firm the steps of those who delight in him; though they may stumble, they will not fall, for the Lord upholds them with his hand." (Psalm 37:23-24) Whether we were learning presence through structure or through freedom, life's richness was found not in rushing through it, but in being fully awake for whatever moment God had given us.

Perhaps that was the real gift both our communities offered: the understanding that true strength came not from speed, but from depth. Whether standing watch over Chesapeake Bay or watching great-grandchildren chase butterflies, the blessing was the same—complete presence in whatever moment we had been given.

Amazing Grace Challenge

Practice being fully present in one daily routine you usually rush through. Whether it's morning coffee, an evening walk, or a phone call with family, bring the same attention a child gives to examining flowers. Notice what beauty reveals when you stop hurrying long enough to really see.

Today I witnessed Grace when:

Divine Whispers from the Patio

♥

Parkview at Touchmark in Edmond, OK. Tramba patio in the background. Photo Credit: Norm Tramba.

Be still, and know that I am God. —Psalm 46:10 (NIV)

There's a sacred space in my life that requires no walls or roof—my back patio. It's here, surrounded by God's artistry, that I often find myself most centered and connected to what truly matters.

This morning was no exception. As I settled into my favorite Amish rocker, the sunshine wrapped around me like a warm embrace. The fountains near our gazebo provided their steady, soothing rhythm—nature's meditation soundtrack, inviting me to slow down, breathe more deeply, and pray with intention rather than haste.

As I sank into this peaceful state, my phone buzzed with a notification. Usually, these digital interruptions pull me away from present moments; however, today was different. Our son's Bird Buddy camera had captured a stunning cardinal, its vibrant red plumage a vivid splash of color against the morning light. I wondered if Grandmother Donovan was visiting.

And then, as if orchestrated by divine timing, a hummingbird appeared at our flower bed. It hovered near the blooms, wings beating so rapidly they blurred into near invisibility. I watched, transfixed, as this tiny miracle suspended itself in midair, drawing sustenance from the nectar.

In that moment of quiet observation, something profound settled over me. A gentle understanding that transcended words. God was speaking through His creation, and for once, I was still enough to listen.

How often do I rush from one task to the next, missing these small but significant divine invitations! The hummingbird, pausing to refresh itself with nectar, became a living metaphor for my spiritual journey. Just as this delicate creature needs nectar for sustenance, my soul thirsts for God's presence—the energy source that sustains me through daily challenges and joys.

My thoughts and prayers drift to Gracelyn in Anapolis. She's probably been up for hours, marching in formation, embracing the disciplined activities her training demands. Does she find time to pause and soak in the beauty of the birds our God creates, or does her rigorous schedule leave little room for such sacred moments?

Yet perhaps that's precisely why these whispers matter so much. In seasons of intense discipline and in seasons of slowing down, we all need reminders to be nourished by God's presence. The hummingbird's visit was a tiny messenger delivering an essential truth: pausing to experience God isn't a luxury when time permits—it's a vital discipline that transforms how we move through our days.

Whether we're 18 and learning military precision or 80 and learning the art of stillness, God speaks through the simplest elements of His creation. The question isn't whether He's communicating, but whether we're positioning ourselves to listen.

May we have the wisdom to recognize these divine whispers in our daily lives, the discipline to create space for sacred stillness, and the grace to trust that God speaks through the smallest moments when we position ourselves to listen.

Amazing Grace Challenge

Create your own sacred space—whether it's a patio chair, a park bench, or even a comfortable spot by a window. Spend 15 minutes there each day this week without any agenda except to notice God's creation around you.

Put your phone aside and practice the discipline of stillness. Pay attention to what small messages He might send your way and listen for His voice.

Today I witnessed Grace when:

Like Grandma, Like Granddaughter

Celebrating Gracelyn at Fireside Restaurant in OKC. Photo Credit: Todd Tramba.

He gives strength to the weary and increases the power of the weak. — Isaiah 40:29 (NIV)

There I was, tackling the chaos that had become my office with newfound determination. I sorted through books, particularly that towering stack of "someday I'll read these" novels that had been giving me guilt pangs for months. With great satisfaction, I packed them into a box and strategically placed it by my recliner for easy access.

The universe has a sense of humor. Within minutes, I managed to trip spectacularly over my box of literary ambitions, resulting in a fractured metatarsal and a sprained ankle. Talk about adding insult to injury—literally tripped up by my own good intentions! But here's the silver lining: now I have doctor's orders to sit in my recliner, elevate my foot, and read all those books. Sometimes life forces us to do precisely what we've been putting off.

Then comes the unexpected twist. While browsing the Naval Academy website, there she is in a photo—our tough-as-nails granddaughter, Gracelyn, sporting a splint on her left leg. I had to laugh despite my concern. She's inherited more than just the color of my eyes and love of adventure; apparently, she's got my talent for spectacular timing when it comes to minor disasters.

The irony isn't lost on me. Here's Gracelyn, marching, running, and doing push-ups that would make a Marine weep, while I'm conquering the challenging terrain between my kitchen and living room. She probably earned her injury through some demanding feat of military training, while I was defeated by a cardboard box and my own two feet.

Yet in our shared predicament, I discover something profound: we're both learning to find strength we didn't know we had. She's battling the rigors of Plebe summer while learning to push through pain. I'm learning that sometimes the most incredible adventures happen when you're forced to slow down and discover what's right in front of you—like a stack of unread books just waiting to transport you to other worlds.

The hardest part? Gracelyn has no phone access during Plebe summer. I can't call to compare war stories or tell her that her accident-prone grandmother is thinking of her and praying for her recovery. She has to tough it out surrounded by her fellow midshipmen, while I get to recuperate with Papa Norm as my personal nurse and chief worrywart.

But you know what runs in families? Resilience. The ability to find humor in mishaps. The determination to make the best of unexpected detours. As I sit here with my elevated foot, reading those long-neglected novels, I'm reminded that sometimes our greatest limitations become our most surprising gifts. And somewhere in Maryland, a young woman with my stubborn streak and accident-prone tendencies is learning the same lesson in her own way.

We may be separated by distance and circumstances, but we're both discovering that grace—whether aging with it or growing into it—often comes through the very challenges we never see coming. May we find the strength to endure unexpected challenges, the grace to accept help from others, and the wisdom to see how our limitations can become unexpected gifts.

Like family traits passed down through generations, resilience and humor may be our greatest inheritance to share.

Amazing Grace Challenge

When life throws you a curveball, practice the "silver lining search." Write down three unexpected benefits that could emerge from your current challenge or limitation. Maybe that injury means more time for a neglected hobby, or perhaps it's an opportunity to let others care for you. Sometimes our constraints become doorways to gifts we never anticipated. I call my accident a God Pause that He knew I needed.

Today I witnessed Grace when:

His Eye Is on the Sparrow

Connie cradling a tiny sparrow in Greensburg, Kansas. (1988)
Photo Credit: Marion Livengood.

Look at the birds of the air; they neither sow nor reap
nor gather into barns, and yet your heavenly Father
feeds them. Are you not of more value than they?
—Matthew 6:26 (NIV)

The framed photograph in my office holds more than a family memory—it captures a profound truth about God's tender care. Uncle Marion Livengood snapped this picture in 1988, showing my cousin Connie cradling a tiny sparrow, a cheerful Band-Aid wrapped around her small thumb. That simple band-aid speaks volumes about compassion and divine protection working hand in hand.

Living in our retirement community means confronting life's fragility on a daily basis. Friends relocate to be near family, transition to higher levels of care, or face inevitable health challenges. Hip fractures, cardiac episodes, and sudden strokes touch lives we know intimately. For the first time, I find myself attending more memorial services than weddings or anniversaries. In solitary moments, the question whispers: Will I be the next one?

When anxiety threatens to overwhelm, I turn my chair toward that treasured photograph. The image draws me to Christ's reassuring words:

"Look at the birds of the air; they neither sow nor reap nor gather into barns, and yet your heavenly Father feeds them. Are you not of more value than they?" (Matthew 6:26)

Sometimes the magnitude of this world makes it difficult to believe I truly matter, yet this simple truth offers profound comfort. God's watchful eye encompasses everything—from life's monumental moments to the most minor details, like a band-aid on a child's thumb.

My prayers naturally turn to our children and grandchildren, with Gracelyn holding a special place in my heart during her challenging first year at the Naval Academy. Academy life demands resilience I can barely imagine. At the Academy, attention to detail matters—just as God's attentiveness to small things reminds us that if He notices when a sparrow falls, He certainly sees our daily struggles and joys.

As I observe the sparrows and robins frequenting our backyard, I wonder what birds Gracelyn encounters in Annapolis. Perhaps pelicans, like those she photographed during her NAPS year. It brings me peace to know that the same God who cares for the birds outside my window also watches over Gracelyn. Though we cannot be physically present with her, our Heavenly Father never leaves her side.

Prayer hasn't always come naturally to me. Worry sometimes creates barriers between my heart and God, leaving me speechless when I most need to speak. During those difficult seasons, I've discovered strength in interceding for others. At the Naval Academy, midshipmen learn that perseverance doesn't always require feeling confident; sometimes it means showing up despite uncertainty.

The challenge of loving someone from a distance—whether a grandchild at the Naval Academy or a friend who has moved away—teaches us about faith in God's omnipresence. When we cannot be physically present with our loved ones, we can trust that God's presence never wavers. His care extends beyond geographical boundaries and time zones.

We participate in God's network of care that spans across communities, generations, and institutions, such as the Naval Academy. Midshipmen learn that they are part of something larger than themselves—a long line of graduates who support one another throughout their careers. This tradition mirrors the body of Christ, where each person's prayers and care strengthen the whole community.

When we pray for others, we become instruments of His care, strengthening those we love while drawing closer to His heart. We can lift their names in prayer, trusting that even when we lack specific details, God sees what remains invisible to us. Together, we create a network of support, weaving our shared concerns into a beautiful tapestry of faith and hope.

May God enfold them in His unfailing love, grant them peace that surpasses understanding, and remind them of His constant presence. Like the sparrow safely held in caring hands, may we rest in the certainty that our Heavenly Father's eye is always upon us.

Amazing Grace Challenge

Remember that every person whose life touches yours—from the dining room staff to fellow residents, from midshipmen to distant relatives—can benefit from being held in prayer.

Take time to consider the hidden struggles surrounding you—friends masking pain behind smiles, family members facing private battles, neighbors carrying burdens you may never know. Be an intercessor and pray for someone you've been worried about, letting them know they are in your thoughts and prayers.

Today I witnessed Grace when:

The Blessing of Small Things

♥

Smudge catching a snowball. He brought joy to their family and is now in Rainbow Heaven. Photo credit: Somer Tramba.

Give thanks in all circumstances; for this is God's will for you in Christ Jesus. —1 Thessalonians 5:18 (NIV)

Today would have been my brother Dennis's birthday. The calendar reminds me of that gentle ache that comes when someone you love becomes a memory instead of a phone call.

Dennis left us last year, joining my cousin Terry, who was taken far too young at nineteen, and the growing collection of souls who have shaped my heart—my parents, classmates, neighbors, and dear friends who completed their earthly journey ahead of me.

Living in a retirement community, I'm among those who know the losses that come with aging—names crossed out in address books, photo albums filled with memories. Yet, these experiences remind us to treasure what we still have.

When I think about death—not morbidly, but honestly—I find myself asking: What small joys would I miss if I weren't here tomorrow? Surprisingly, it's rarely the big-ticket items that come to mind. Not the awards gathering dust on shelves or the houses we've owned or the impressive accomplishments we've accumulated. Instead, it's the humble, everyday miracles that would break my heart to leave behind.

I would miss that first sip of coffee in the morning, steam rising like a small prayer from my favorite mug. I'd miss hearing Norm talking to himself in his office, and how we've perfected the art of comfortable silence when we are together. Usually we discover we were thinking about the same things. These moments aren't Instagram-worthy, but they're life-worthy.

I would miss the morning bird symphony outside my window—better than any concert I've attended. I'd miss the way afternoon sunlight sneaks through the blinds and warms my reading chair, creating the perfect spot for both naps and novels. God's daily light show of sunrise and sunset would go unwitnessed by these old eyes, and what a tragedy that would be.

I would miss the sound of rain drumming against the window while I'm safe and warm inside, and the satisfaction of turning the last page of a book that's transported me to places I'll never visit in person. I'd miss the way my grandchildren's voices change when they call—growing deeper, more confident, more themselves with each conversation.

Speaking of grandchildren, I would miss tracking Gracelyn's Naval Academy adventures from afar, wondering if she's remembering to eat well and whether she's making friends who appreciate her wonderful, stubborn spirit. I'd miss not knowing how her story unfolds, what uniform she'll wear with pride, and which hearts she'll touch along the way.

I would miss the simple pleasure of a cool breeze on a hot Oklahoma day, the way ice cream tastes better when shared, and the satisfaction of finally organizing that one drawer that's been bothering me for months. I'd miss the luxury of a hot shower and the comfort of my favorite blanket during evening TV time with Norm.

Most of all, I would miss the connections—the way a neighbor's smile can brighten a cloudy day, the warmth of a hug that says more than words ever could, and the blessed feeling of belonging somewhere, of being known and loved for exactly who I am, with all my wrinkles and quirks.

In our productivity-obsessed world, we often sprint past these gentle gifts, our minds churning with to-do lists and tomorrow's worries. But the losses in my life have taught me that noticing these small blessings isn't just about cultivating gratitude—it's about recognizing God's fingerprints on ordinary moments. When we pause to say "thank you" for morning coffee and evening stars, we're not just being polite; we're practicing worship.

The apostle, Paul, was familiar with loss and hardship, yet he encouraged us to give thanks in all circumstances. Not for all circumstances—because grief and loss aren't cause for celebration—but in them, finding threads of grace woven through even our darkest seasons.

Dennis was the kind of person who noticed small things: a cardinal at the bird feeder, the way squirrels scampered across telephone wires. In missing him, I'm learning to see the world through his appreciative eyes, finding him in every small joy I pause to acknowledge. Perhaps that's how love transcends loss—by teaching us to notice what we might otherwise overlook.

May we develop eyes to see God's daily gifts in the ordinary moments, hearts grateful for simple pleasures, and the wisdom to recognize that the smallest blessings often carry the greatest joy. Like Dennis, may we become people who notice the beautiful details that make life precious.

Amazing Grace Challenge

Write down each day this week ordinary moments from your day that brought joy, and when you witnessed Grace. Perhaps the taste of your morning coffee, a kind word from a friend, or the way light fell across your kitchen table.

At the week's end, read through your entries and notice how many ways God showed up in the seemingly mundane. Thank God for these grace moments and consider sharing these blessings with a parent, grandchild or friend.

Today I witnessed Grace when:

Grandmother and Roses: God's Masterpiece

♥

Grandma Dana and her roses. Photo Credit: Norm Tramba.

For, All people are like grass, and all their glory is like the flowers of the field; the grass withers and the flowers fall. —1 Peter 1:24 (NIV)

My Grandma Shara seemed ancient when I was a child. She lived in Narka, Kansas, about a four-hour drive from our farm. Mom was thoughtful about visits—she never wanted Grandma to fuss, so she never announced our arrival ahead of time.

When we drove through Belleville, we would stop at a payphone to give an hour of warning. "I want to give her a little time," Mom would say, "so she doesn't see us and have a heart attack."

We only visited her a few times a year, but every visit meant sleeping with Grandma on her big feather mattress—sinking into it like floating on a cloud.

When we reached her home, we walked up the curved sidewalk to her front porch. There was no grass in her yard, just a cottage garden bursting with flowers. Giant peonies nodded in the breeze, lilac bushes surrounded the home, daisies dotted the beds, and climbing red roses cascaded over the side of the porch. Like all Kansas gardens, hers boasted sunflowers that towered above my head. But Grandma had one rule: "Leave them alone so that everyone can enjoy them." The neighbors told us that she would often bring out her accordion and play on the porch in the evenings, creating an end-of-day ritual that they all treasured.

Her home always carried the warm scent of yeast from the kolaches and bread loaves perpetually baking in her oven. The backyard was Grandma's working sanctuary, enclosed by a fence and filled with chickens of every color imaginable. She collected eggs to sell at the store, saving every penny to send her daughters to college.

Mom and Aunt Lee became the first women from Narka to attend university, both became teachers, thanks to Grandma's egg money—a quiet revolution funded by daily acts of love. Mom attended K-State at age 16 and graduated in 1932.

This legacy of quiet investment reminds me of our investment in Gracelyn at the Naval Academy. Just as Grandma Shara's daily care of her chickens funded education that changed her daughters' lives, we're investing in Grace's future through our prayers, letters, and support. The Academy teaches midshipmen that excellence comes through small, consistent actions—perfectly pressed uniforms, precise attention to detail, daily choices to serve something greater than themselves.

Grandma Shara understood this long before the Naval Academy codified it into military doctrine. Her philosophy of tending beautiful gardens "so that everyone can enjoy them" mirrors what Gracelyn is learning about service and sacrifice. Both women, generations apart, discovered that the most meaningful contributions often happen quietly, through faithful stewardship of whatever gifts and opportunities God provides.

As Grandma Shara aged, the family eventually found her a care home where she spent her remaining years. I was attending nursing school when Mom called to tell me Grandma had passed away. She didn't want me to attend the funeral, thinking it more important for me to stay and take my finals.

That night, I had a dream about Grandma Shara. She was busy helping other angels tend the flower gardens in heaven.

Now I wonder what Gracelyn will think of me, her Grandma Dana. She'll have memories of a grandmother who moved across the country to see her grandchildren more than three times a year. A Grandma who loved her unconditionally but expressed her feelings more effectively in writing than in conversation. Perhaps she'll remember birthday celebrations and quiet moments of connection across the generations.

I imagine Gracelyn might picture me in heaven, line dancing with friends and tending all the animals I've loved in my life—just as I see Grandma Shara among her eternal flowers. Maybe by then, Grace will understand that love expresses itself differently across generations, but the investment in each other's growth remains constant.

Every bloom in Grandma's garden was one of God's masterpieces, as was Grandma Shara herself, and as are our children and grandchildren. How blessed we are to be part of a family, especially when our children reach out to show they care by helping us find safe harbor in life's final season.

May we follow Grandma Shara's example of quiet generosity, finding ways to invest in future generations through small, consistent acts of love. Like flowers in a cottage garden, may our legacy bloom in unexpected ways, bringing beauty and nourishment to those who come after us.

Amazing Grace Challenge

Like Grandma Shara's egg money that funded education, identify one small, consistent action you can take this week to invest in a younger family member's future. It may be setting aside a dollar a day for a grandchild's education, teaching a skill, writing down family stories they'll treasure someday, or simply sending an encouraging note.

Your daily acts of love might create ripple effects across generations, just as Grandma's chickens helped create teachers who shaped countless young minds.

Today I witnessed Grace when:

Our Prayer Walk

♥

Desert Botanical Garden. Photo Credit: Wikimedia Commons.

The heavens declare the glory of God; the skies proclaim the work of his hands. —Psalm 19:1 (NIV)

A day trip can refresh the soul like nothing else. Living in Arizona, when I need a break from writing, Norm and I drive to the Desert Botanical Garden in Phoenix. Within twenty minutes, we can immerse ourselves in the beauty of the Arizona desert—God's masterpiece spread before us.

"Look, Dana, at that majestic saguaro," Norm points out. "It takes seventy years before they grow their first arm."

We watch as a cactus wren hops around the towering cactus, scanning the horizon before darting into the dark hole that serves as its nest. The sight strikes me as a metaphor for my own life. I am as old as that saguaro, with over seventy years of memories waiting to be written. Like the wren, I pause to survey my surroundings—writing in my gratitude journal, looking back on life. Sometimes, like that bird, I want to retreat into the safe darkness, resting with stories from the more difficult chapters of my past.

We continue down the meandering path, pausing under the filtered shade of a Palo Verde tree. The desert is alive with color—painted lady butterflies dance around purple blooms, creating a living kaleidoscope. Hummingbirds dart to the coral fountain, sipping nectar before disappearing as quickly as they appeared.

Further along, a desert tortoise travels steadily down the dirt path, wholly focused on its destination and oblivious to our presence. The sight reminds me of the fable about the tortoise and the hare. I wonder, if I stay focused and work consistently, little by little, will I finally finish my memoir?

The valley spreads before us, blanketed in shades of red. Organ pipe cacti reach toward the sky, while barrel cacti at their base show off brilliant purple blooms. We know the summer monsoon rain will soon arrive to calm the restless dust devils swirling up from the earth.

Like these dry desert paths, I occasionally hit periods of drought in my writing. Like the desert itself, it takes time to emerge from these barren seasons. But when the rain finally comes, it's exhilarating and refreshing—the desert blooms in glorious response. Ideas flow freely, and there are periods of unstoppable writing, words pouring onto the page like life-giving water.

I think of Gracelyn during her morning runs at the Naval Academy. Even in that structured environment, I wonder if she experiences seasons that feel like drought—times when the demands feel overwhelming. I hope she occasionally slows her pace to absorb the beauty around her, rather than just focusing on beating her previous time. There are too many gifts in our world to rush past. We need to slow down and savor the journey.

Our journey feels like a prayer walk as we conclude our day trip. God's world surrounds us everywhere, and He meets us in nature, touching us with gentle breezes—His gift to us. Whether it's the ocean, mountains, flat plains, or desert, whether it's birds and butterflies in our backyard, His presence can be felt.

A prayer walk offers a unique way to sense God's presence. He sees us enjoying His beautiful creation and serenades us with nature's symphony. Walking hand in hand with your loved one makes the journey perfect. These moments of connection with creation remind us that even in our golden years, we can find renewal and inspiration in the simple act of paying attention to the world around us.

May we learn to see each walk as a prayer, each moment in nature as communion with our Creator, and each season of our lives—whether blooming or resting—as part of God's perfect design. Like the desert after rain, may we trust that our dry seasons will give way to unexpected bursts of beauty and growth.

Amazing Grace Challenge

Like the focused desert tortoise, choose one meaningful project or goal you've been putting off. Commit to making steady, small progress each day this week—no rushing, just consistent forward movement while staying present to the beauty along the way. Let the tortoise teach you that persistence, not speed, often leads to the most meaningful destinations.

Today I witnessed Grace when:

Today's Technology and Heaven's Hotline

Dana with her technology. Photo Credit: Norm Tramba.

Call me and I will answer you and tell you great and unsearchable things you do not know. —Jeremiah 33:3 (NIV)

Technology has transformed our world beyond childhood imagination. My siblings and I learned to navigate the old party-line telephone, listening for our specific ring pattern amid shared rural conversations. The contrast struck me during a recent trip to Branson with my thirteen-year-old grandson, Elijah. While Norm and I struggled with our car's GPS, Eli effortlessly operated his device from the back seat, an Australian voice confidently guiding us as we fumbled with buttons.

I have welcomed technology into my daily routine, discovering unexpected joy in reconnecting with classmates from 1966 on Facebook—friends who shared nearly two decades of our lives in our small Kansas town. Social media brings both celebration and sorrow with startling immediacy. I delight in pictures of births, weddings, pets, and growing children, but I also face obituaries that remind me of life's seasons of loss.

The double-edged nature of technology became clear during our recent trip home. Within minutes, my phone displayed a cascade of heavy news: friends facing cancer diagnoses, neighbors moving to hospice, and heartbreaking updates about desperate treatments. News that once took days to arrive now comes instantly, sometimes overwhelming me.

Yet technology reveals its redemptive power in moments of crisis. When childhood friend Boni received her cancer diagnosis, I posted a prayer request on Facebook. Within hours, over a hundred friends worldwide were lifting her name up to God. The same technology that inundates me with bad news can also mobilize prayer warriors more quickly than ever.

This sharply contrasts with my childhood, when news of a neighbor's hardship might have taken weeks to reach us. Now, I can respond immediately with support, prayers, and encouragement. I can instantly text Gracelyn at the Naval Academy and receive a heart emoji back, knowing she's busy but okay.

At the Academy, technology serves purposes far different from our retirement years. Where we maintain connections with the past and share life's joys and sorrows, midshipmen master sophisticated radar, navigation, and communication systems that will protect our nation. They're learning to operate advanced warfare technology that requires precision and split-second decision-making.

Even in their high-tech environment, these young people need the same timeless connection that has sustained every military generation—a direct prayer line to God. When Gracelyn faces exam pressure, leadership challenges, or uncertainty about future assignments, I pray she remembers that the most vital communication system requires no Wi-Fi or satellites.

Every Wednesday, I gather with friends who share life stories and pray for those in need. We exchange updates about grandchildren, share concerns for our community, and connect with our Heavenly Father as prayer warriors for friends and family near and far.

Prayer works anytime, anywhere, regardless of signal strength or battery life. When my heart bears concern for sick friends, our troubled world, or our grandchildren and children, I can call instantly. His line is never busy, He never sends me to voicemail, and He always has time to listen.

The beautiful irony is striking. The old party line required careful listening for ring patterns and waiting for turns to speak. Today's technology demands passwords, Wi-Fi, and constant updates. The Naval Academy operates with sophisticated encrypted communications. But my heavenly hotline—the most important connection—requires no codes, fees, or service interruptions.

While I am grateful for technology that helps me stay connected worldwide, including with my precious granddaughter, who is learning to serve her country, I am even more thankful for the eternal connection that needs no upgrades or technical support. The same God who heard my grandmother's prayers—who had no telephone—hears mine through the most advanced communication system ever created. And He hears Gracelyn's prayers, too, whether she's walking through Bancroft Hall or standing watch on future naval vessels.

Amazing Grace Challenge

In a world of constantly changing technology, remember you have a hotline to your Father in Heaven that never needs updating. Use it daily, knowing He's always available.

Whether praying for grandchildren facing new challenges, friends battling illness, or seeking guidance in your daily journey, God's communication system never fails. Have you used His hotline today?

Today I witnessed Grace when:

Let There Be Peace on Earth

Touchmark in Coffee Creek. (Edmond, Oklahoma)
Photo Credit: Norm Tramba.

*Peace I leave with you; my peace I give you. I do not
give to you as the world gives. Do not let your hearts be
troubled and do not be afraid.* —John 14:27 (NIV)

On November 22, 1963, I was sixteen years old, playing
saxophone with my fellow band members in the Lewis, Kansas,
High School gymnasium. We were practicing "Time Out for
a Jam Session" when Mr. Warren O'Connor, our principal,
solemnly descended the stairs between the bleachers. His
unexpected interruption brought our music to an abrupt halt.

With a grave expression that I can still see clearly today, he
announced, "Our President, John F. Kennedy, has just been
assassinated in Dallas, Texas."

The silence that followed felt deafening. Then Mr. Johnson,
our band director, raised his baton and spoke with unmistakable
certainty: "You will never forget what you were doing, at this
moment, on this day, when you heard about your President's
assassination."

Tears welled in my eyes as the reality settled over our small
gymnasium. True to his prediction, those moments remain
etched in my memory with perfect clarity —the feel of the
saxophone in my hands, the echo of our interrupted song, the
weight of tragedy descending upon our innocent world.

In those days, the Cold War wasn't just political theory—it
was a palpable presence in our daily lives. At school, we practiced
drills for both bombs and tornadoes. Many Americans lived in
genuine fear that Soviet leader Nikita Khrushchev might launch
an attack at any moment.

My mother couldn't sleep for days following Kennedy's
assassination. "I keep hearing the drum cadence," she confided,
"and seeing visions of the casket drawn by those white horses."
Now, as both a mother and grandmother myself, I understand
her profound distress. We instinctively yearn for the world to be

safe for our children and grandchildren—a universal prayer that transcends political affiliations and generations.

Meanwhile, halfway around the world, Norm was serving in the Air Force on the island of Okinawa. He worked on a seven-man launch crew for four Mace Missiles, serving as the airframe and engine mechanic. Among his most serious duties was connecting the nuclear warhead—the final step in arming each missile for potential launch. He still speaks quietly about the weight of that responsibility, knowing he was working with nuclear weapons far more powerful than those that devastated Hiroshima and Nagasaki.

Those were different times, yet the fundamental calling to serve remains unchanged. Today I think of Gracelyn and her fellow midshipmen at the Naval Academy, preparing to serve our country in an equally complex world. While we faced nuclear war, they confront cyber warfare, terrorism, and global instability. But like Norm's generation, they're learning that true strength lies not in the ability to wage war, but in the wisdom to prevent it.

At the Academy, Gracelyn walks halls where generations of naval officers learned that military service has always been about more than weapons and warfare—it's about being guardians of peace through strength. The Navy's mission of maintaining freedom of navigation speaks to something deeper: the belief that open seas lead to open dialogue, that nations connected by trade are less likely to be divided by conflict.

Within our retirement community, we represent a diverse range of political perspectives and life experiences. Among our friends are a four-star general, a former POW, and veterans from every branch of service. We have Democrats and Republicans. Despite these differences, we've discovered something beautiful: we share a common aspiration for a safe and prosperous world. We've learned to coexist harmoniously, honoring our differences while celebrating our shared humanity.

This daily example of peaceful coexistence gives me hope. If we can achieve harmony in our small community, perhaps Gracelyn's generation can do the same on a larger scale. Every port they visit, every international exercise, every humanitarian mission becomes an opportunity to demonstrate that strength and compassion can coexist.

Years later, when Norm and I visited the John F. Kennedy Presidential Library in Boston, I purchased a simple metal sign bearing words that captured my heart: "O God, Thy sea is so great, and my boat is so small." This ancient sailor's prayer resonates deeply as I contemplate the weight of history and pray for the world our grandchildren will inherit.

The prayer reminds us that while we may feel small upon God's great sea, we each have a part to play in steering toward peace. As we journey through our golden years, carrying wisdom earned through decades of joy and sorrow, may we choose to build bridges rather than walls, to seek understanding rather than victory.

Amazing Grace Challenge

The ancient sailor's prayer echoes in our hearts: "O God, Thy sea is so great, and my boat is so small." Yet perhaps that's exactly where peace begins—with the humble recognition that while we cannot control the vastness of the ocean, we can choose the direction of our own small vessel.

This week, practice one small act of bridge-building in your community. Listen to someone whose views differ from yours. Show kindness to someone who needs it. Choose understanding over judgment. Peace may begin with you.

Today I witnessed Grace when:

From Party Lines to Community Bonds

Donovan phone from Centerview, Kansas farm.
Photo Credit: Norm Tramba.

Be still, and know that I am God. —Psalm 46:10 (NIV)

One afternoon when I was eight years old, Mom ran an errand to town, leaving us kids home alone. We let our green parakeet Bing out of her cage, and she promptly flew behind the chest freezer, trapped in the narrow space between the appliance and the wall. We crawled on top, trying to shoo her out with a yardstick, our panic growing with each failed attempt.

Finally, we called Lenora Bratcher, our wise neighbor. Through our old wall phone's crackling connection, Lenora's calm voice delivered unexpected advice: "Leave the parakeet alone, honey. She'll find her own way out when she's ready."

We wanted to do something—anything—but Lenora insisted we simply wait. Hours later, as we sat quietly at the kitchen table, Bing emerged on her own and flew straight back to her cage.

That parakeet taught me something I'm still learning decades later: not every problem requires immediate action. Sometimes the strongest response is patient trust.

This lesson feels especially relevant as I watch our granddaughter Gracelyn navigate life at the Naval Academy. In military training, she's learning to assess situations carefully before acting—that wisdom often whispers, "Wait and watch before you move." The Academy teaches that hasty decisions in military leadership can have serious consequences, so midshipmen practice the discipline of thoughtful response rather than reactive rushing.

I imagine her facing moments of uncertainty—academic pressure, leadership challenges, homesickness—when every instinct might urge immediate action. But like Lenora's advice about the parakeet, sometimes the wisest course is to be still, trust the process, and allow time for clarity to emerge.

Here in our retirement community, I see the same principle at work. We're surrounded by neighbors rich in experience, ready to offer counsel when asked. Many of us have learned through decades of living that our most frantic worries often resolve themselves when we stop chasing solutions and create space for wisdom to unfold.

Whether it's concern about a health issue that needs time for proper diagnosis, worry about a grandchild who needs space to work through their own challenges, or anxiety about changes we cannot control, we're discovering that being still doesn't mean being passive—it means trusting God's timing over our urgency.

The transition to retirement living itself required this kind of patient trust. Moving from our longtime homes, adjusting to new routines, building new friendships—none of it happened overnight. Like that parakeet finding her way out from behind the freezer, we each discovered our path to belonging in this community when the time was right.

I think of all the times I've rushed toward solutions that weren't yet ready to be found. All the worries I've carried that eventually worked themselves out, all the problems I've tried to solve that simply needed time to ripen into clarity. Lenora's eight-year-old wisdom still rings true: sometimes the kindest thing we can do for ourselves and others is to stop flailing and trust that the way forward will reveal itself.

Whether we're eight years old with a trapped bird, twenty years old facing the pressures of military training, or eighty years old adjusting to new limitations, the principle remains constant. In our rushing world, God's timing often requires us to be still first. The parakeet eventually found her way out. Gracelyn is finding her way through academy challenges. And we're finding our way through the transitions of aging—all in their proper season, all when the time is right.

Amazing Grace Challenge

When facing problems this week, resist the urge to spring into action immediately. Remember Bing the parakeet—sometimes the wisest solution emerges when we step back, breathe deeply, and trust God's timing. Practice being still before being busy. Let patience be your first response, not your last resort.

Today I witnessed Grace when:

Finding Grace in
Making Someday Today

♥

Gracelyn at Naval Academy Preparatory School in Newport,
RI. (2024) Photo Credit: NAPS.

Commit to the Lord whatever you do, and He will establish your plans. —Proverbs 16:3 (NIV)

"You know what I regret most?" I shared with my friend Boni over lunch in our retirement community dining room. "Years ago, I lacked the courage to follow my own dreams. I always enjoyed writing, and I wanted to join the Air Force and become a flight nurse." I let my "someday" slip away.

I spent my first forty years rushing through life, living by what society expected of me. As a young woman in the 1960s, I had few choices: teacher, nurse, secretary, or housewife. I chose nursing, then became a busy mom, working while raising children. I worked hard and saved money for retirement, but often forgot to savor the special moments along the way. My "someday" was always just around the corner: someday I'll write that book, someday I'll search for my birth family.

Now, looking back, I wish I had followed my dreams instead of perpetually waiting for "someday." Perhaps this is the time to pursue those dreams I've been putting off—and to encourage others, including my granddaughter Grace, to do the same.

The thought sparked something in me. I signed up for a writing course with Richard Crum, a former National Geographic editor to improve my skills. As I continued to write, I discovered the gift I had carried inside me for decades. My memoir, *Making Peace With The Pieces of My Life*, was published on my 75th birthday. I thought to myself, "I can't believe I waited so long."

This message feels especially important for Gracelyn at the Naval Academy. While she's following a structured path now, I hope she remembers that even within discipline and duty, there's room for personal dreams. The Academy teaches leadership and service, but it also shapes individuals who will one day have their own "somedays" to pursue.

I want her to know: Today is yesterday's tomorrow. The "someday" we've been waiting for is here now. Each day is like a blank page waiting to be written. What joy might she find by embracing both her naval calling and her personal passions? When working for others, remember you're also working for God. Use your gifts and develop into the person He meant you to be.

Here in our retirement community, I see daily examples of people making "someday" today. A retired four-star general and his wife launched a nonprofit leadership camp, shaping future leaders. Fellow residents found their calling as museum docents, sharing their passion for history with others. Many others have discovered meaningful ways to serve—some sewing comfort items for hospitalized children, others becoming prayer warriors for our community and families.

Each person has transformed years of accumulated wisdom and experience into a present-day purpose. Their "someday I'll make a difference" became "today I am making a difference."

What postponed dreams can you pursue now, adapted to your current season? Age brings limitations, but also freedoms we didn't have in youth—freedom from the pressure to be perfect, freedom to try new things without worrying about career implications, freedom to focus on what truly brings joy.

Recently, I thanked my writing mentor for believing in me when I didn't believe in myself. He was grateful for my words. That exchange reminded me that gratitude is a gift that blesses both giver and receiver.

As we age, we gain something invaluable—we begin to see what truly matters. Let's use this wisdom by making each day count. One small step can significantly change our tomorrow. Someday is not a destination; it's a decision—a decision to stop waiting for perfect circumstances and start embracing the possibility that our someday is today.

Amazing Grace Challenge

Create a "Living Fully Now" list rather than a distant bucket list. Focus on achievable experiences that bring joy and purpose, then commit to acting on one each month.

My list includes simple pleasures: writing handwritten letters, welcoming new friends as they move into our community, and spending every opportunity I can with our sons and grandchildren.

For Grace at the Academy, her "Living Fully Now" list might include seeking genuine conversations with professors beyond classroom requirements or learning one completely unrelated skill each semester that brings pure joy without the pressure of grades.

What's on your list?

Today I witnessed Grace when:

Coming Home: Easter Reflections on Faith, Hope, and God's Perfect Timing

♥

Photo Credit: Wikimedia Commons.

*"For I know the plans I have for you," declares the
Lord, "plans to prosper you and not to harm you, to
give you hope and a future."*—Jeremiah 29:11 (NIV)

As April blooms with new life, Norm and I eagerly prepare
for a meaningful homecoming. After more than thirty years
away, we're returning to Clearwater, Kansas, where I've been
invited to speak at an Easter breakfast. The invitation fills me
with excitement and nostalgia—how can three decades have
passed since we last walked those familiar streets and called that
close-knit community our home?

Clearwater holds a sacred place in our hearts. It's where we
raised our boys, Troy and Todd, where our faith was tested and
ultimately strengthened. Sometimes, the places that shape us
most profoundly are the ones we must leave behind to fully
understand their impact.

This homecoming has me reflecting on how God works
behind the scenes in ways we can't see or understand. We
thought we were in control then, making our plans and charting
our path. However, God had something entirely different in
mind. Over the years, I've learned that our struggles often
become our greatest teachers—growth opportunities wrapped
in difficult packages.

Each challenge presents a chance to witness what I've come
to call "God-incidents"—those moments that are too perfectly
timed, too intricately arranged to be mere coincidences.

I think of Gracelyn, facing her own moments of uncertainty
and challenge. While her path is structured and her goals clear,
she, too, will discover that God's timing often differs from
our own expectations. The Academy teaches planning and
precision, but life teaches us that sometimes the most beautiful
outcomes emerge when our carefully laid plans intersect with
divine timing.

My own story of unexpected timing continues to unfold. The COVID pandemic, a time of global uncertainty, cleared my calendar for two years and finally created the space I needed to write my memoir. It was a challenging yet rewarding process, but I always felt God's presence guiding me. The book was published on Amazon on my seventy-fifth birthday—proof that some dreams require decades to ripen.

It took seventy years for God to open the doors for me to share my story with the world. He helped me make peace with the pieces of my life, just as He's helping Grace navigate the demanding pieces of her Academy experience. Both journeys require faith that the timing, however unexpected, is exactly right.

When I look back on our time in Clearwater, I want to thank the friends who walked with us through those years. You prayed for us, supported us, and loved us during difficult times. You were truly Jesus' hands and feet to our family, showing us what grace looks like in action.

Here's something life has taught me: resurrection isn't just about Jesus rising from the tomb on that first Easter morning. It's about resurrection happening in our own lives—hope being restored when all seemed lost, broken relationships being made whole, finding lost dreams while creating new ones.

Think about your own life. Where have you seen God bring new life to something that seemed dead? Where did you find hope when you didn't expect it? Those are your "God-incidents," proof that His timing is always working, even when we can't see it.

As I prepare to return to Clearwater and share my testimony at that Easter breakfast, I'm reminded that homecomings aren't just about returning to a place—they're about recognizing how far we've come and celebrating God's faithfulness through every season.

Whether we're twenty years old at the Naval Academy learning to trust the process, or seventy-five years old reflecting on a lifetime of grace, the message remains the same: God is always writing our stories, and His timing creates endings more beautiful than we could ever imagine.

Amazing Grace Challenge

Keep adding to your Grace Journal, recording those "God-incidents" when His timing was perfect. Include moments when what seemed like delays or detours actually positioned you for something better. Share these with your grandchildren, fellow midshipmen, or family members. Your testimony of God's faithfulness becomes their hope for trusting His timing in their own lives.

Today I witnessed Grace when:

Finding Faith in Simple Things: Lessons from Childhood

♥

Photo Credit: Wikimedia Commons.

He stilled the storm to a whisper; the waves of the sea were hushed. —Psalm 107:29 (NIV)

As a child, I loved our Heavenly Father because the word "father" made me think of my Daddy. Though I never saw him pray outside of meals, those moments stayed with me. I would peek through my almost-closed eyes to see his big, rough, yet gentle hands folded in prayer—hands that could fix anything, gentle enough to hold a newborn calf, strong enough to guide a plow through stubborn soil.

It reminded me of pictures I saw at church of Jesus praying alone in the Garden of Gethsemane. I often wondered about Dad's own prayer time. Did he talk to God while alone in the barn, driving the tractor across endless fields, or watching storm clouds gather during wheat harvest? I like to think these quiet conversations happened while he milked Ole' Bess, with kittens purring around his feet and steam rising from the milk bucket in the cool morning air.

Recent thunderstorms in Oklahoma have brought back vivid memories of those Kansas storms of my childhood. Dad would stand watch by the barn, looking west at the sky. I'd run to his side as we watched clouds build like tall fortresses against the horizon. The sky would change from blue to gray to dark purple, like night coming at noon.

When thunder boomed across the prairie, I'd grab his hand, feeling brave because he was calm. Lightning lit up the land and my father's weathered face, and I felt completely safe—not just because of him, but because of something bigger that he seemed to represent. In those moments, standing beside him while the storm raged, I learned that faith wasn't about having all the answers; it was about trusting in the one who had them. It was about knowing who held us when the winds picked up.

After every storm, we'd walk out together to survey what remained. Sometimes there was damage—broken tree branches, scattered debris, muddy puddles where the yard had been. But Dad always looked beyond the mess to what could be repaired, what could grow again. "Look there," he'd say, pointing to where the sun broke through the clouds. "Storm's moving on."

I think of Gracelyn at the Naval Academy, facing storms of a different kind—the challenge of rigorous training, the pressure of leadership responsibilities, homesickness that strikes without warning. I pray she learned from her father, Todd, what I learned from my father: that the steady hand holding you matters more than the strength of the wind trying to knock you down.

The Academy will teach her to navigate literal storms at sea, to read weather patterns and chart safe courses through turbulent waters. But I hope she also discovers what my father showed me—that the most profound faith often grows not in dramatic moments, but in dependable, quiet ones. In conversations with God that happen not just in chapels, but in dormitory rooms, during evening formation, and in the fellowship of those who understand the weight of service.

As I age, I realize I may have overlooked one of my most important jobs as a grandmother: sharing these simple lessons of faith. Faith doesn't require grand gestures or perfect words. Sometimes it's as simple as standing beside someone you trust while the storm rages, knowing that morning will come.

My father stood watch during Kansas tempests, offering calm strength and pointing toward safety. Now I want to be that reassuring presence for others—and I pray that Gracelyn, in her own way, will become that steady hand for her fellow midshipmen when their storms arrive.

We all long for the same thing after life's tempests pass: God's promise that the waters will recede, the sun will return, and life will continue in all its wonder. Just as my father taught me to look for the break in the clouds, I want Gracelyn to know that every storm eventually moves on, and faith is what carries us through until it does.

Amazing Grace Challenge

This week, be someone's steady presence during their storm. Look for a person in your community who needs a calm hand to hold—perhaps a new resident adjusting to change, a family member facing health challenges, or a friend dealing with loss. Stand watch with them, just as my father stood watch with me, pointing toward hope beyond the current difficulty.

Today I witnessed Grace when:

The Cross in My Window: Lessons in Peacemaking

♥

Photo Credit: Wikimedia Commons.

Blessed are the peacemakers, for they will be called
children of God. —Matthew 5:9 (NIV)

The cross hanging in my office window holds special meaning. It once belonged to my birthmother, who gazed upon it through her final years, perhaps finding comfort in its simple reminder of God's love. Now it serves as my daily symbol of connection across time—a reminder that peace is both deeply personal and beautifully communal.

Peace begins in our own hearts as we accept God's love and extends outward as we offer that same grace to others. But what does this look like in the everyday moments of retirement community living?

In our dining room conversations, when political discussions heat up or when frustrations with neighbors surface, we have choices to make. We can choose to be bridge builders rather than wall builders. When we feel judgmental about someone's habits or critical of their choices, we can remember that we all share the same longing for dignity, understanding, and love.

Gracelyn is learning that military service isn't ultimately about conflict—it's about creating conditions for peace. The Navy's mission includes humanitarian aid, disaster relief, and diplomatic presence around the world. She's discovering that true strength often lies not in the ability to fight, but in the wisdom to prevent fights from happening.

This parallels what we're learning in our golden years: that peacemaking isn't about avoiding disagreement, but about navigating it with grace. We've lived through enough seasons to know that the things dividing us are often temporary, while the things uniting us are eternal.

The beautiful truth about growing older is gaining perspective on what truly matters. We understand that peace is not the absence of conflict, but the presence of grace in the midst of our differences. We can be living examples of Christ's peace, showing others that true strength lies not in being right, but in being loving.

Our parents chose hope over fear when they welcomed children into their homes, even after witnessing the horrors of war. Their choice to love, to build family, to create peace in their small corner of the world—this is how God's kingdom grows, one heart at a time.

Whether through military service like Gracelyn's calling or through quiet acts of daily kindness in our communities, we all have opportunities to be instruments of peace. My prayer is that Gracelyn continues to be a bridge builder, someone with the courage to extend understanding to those who differ from her. And I pray the same for all of us—that peace will flow from our homes and communities into the wider world.

As I look at that cross in my window, I'm reminded that someone before me found comfort in its message. Now it's my turn to carry that peace forward, trusting that others will find hope through our gentle witness of God's love.

Amazing Grace Challenge

This week, practice the discipline of "peaceful pause" before responding in tense moments. When you feel your emotions rising—whether from a political conversation, a frustrating interaction, or community conflict—take three deep breaths and ask yourself: "How can I respond with grace rather than react with judgment?"

Keep track of these moments in your Grace Journal. Notice how this small pause changes not only your response but also the outcome of difficult conversations.

Today I witnessed Grace when:

Fathers Working in Tandem: Potter's Gentle Hands

♥

Troy and Norm Tramba working on model rocket in Clearwater, Kansas. (1983)

Yet you, Lord, are our Father. We are the clay; you are the potter; we are all the work of Your hand. —Isaiah 64:8 (NIV)

When I reflect on this beautiful scripture, I see a pattern that has shaped my entire life: fathers working in partnership with our Heavenly Father to mold each generation with patient love. Like skilled potters who know exactly when to apply pressure and when to allow rest, the father figures in our lives shape us through both their presence and their example.

My Daddy was the first potter in my life, teaching me about unconditional love through his daily faithfulness. His influence didn't end with his death—it continued flowing through the men who learned from his example. When I met Norm, I found someone who, despite losing his father at eighteen months old, had developed that same nurturing spirit through other influences in his life.

Norm has honored Daddy's legacy in unexpected ways, taking over the complex farm paperwork and management that I was supposed to handle after Daddy's passing. His careful stewardship of these details preserves what generations before us built. Through his quiet service, he demonstrates the same dedication that shaped him, now becoming a potter's hand in his own right.

This generational shaping fascinates me. Just as clay must be centered on the wheel before it can be formed, each generation needs the steady influence of faithful fathers to provide that foundation. Then, as the potter's wheel continues turning, those who were shaped become the shapers for the next generation.

I watched this process with our sons, Troy and Todd, as they learned from both Daddy and Norm. Todd, now a contractor, patiently teaches his craft with the same gentle instruction he received. I remember watching him work alongside Gracelyn on home projects, explaining each step with the kind of patience that shapes character as much as it teaches skills. Those moments weren't just about construction—they were about building the steady foundation she would need for whatever challenges lay ahead.

Now Grace is at the Naval Academy, where new father figures have entered her life. The officers and instructors who mentor midshipmen must possess remarkable character themselves to shape young adults who will one day lead our nation. These men and women become temporary potters, applying the pressure of high standards while offering the support that prevents breaking.

I imagine her company officer teaching leadership through example, just as Daddy taught me about love through his daily faithfulness. Her professors challenge her thinking while her fellow midshipmen become brothers and sisters, all part of the shaping process that transforms civilians into naval officers.

In my heart, I see a beautiful partnership: Daddy with God in Heaven, while the living men in our family—Norm, Troy, and Todd—continue the earthly work of shaping hearts and souls. The Academy's father figures join this process, adding their own influence to the clay of her character.

What moves me most is realizing that this potter's wheel never stops turning. God works through faithful fathers across generations, each adding their influence to the shaping of their children. The values my father embodied didn't end with him—they continue flowing through our family line, carried forward by those who learned from his example and now apply those lessons as they guide others.

In our golden years, we have the privilege of watching this beautiful process come full circle. We can see how the father figures who shaped us prepared us to become the potter's hands for others. Whether through parenting, mentoring, or simple acts of guidance, we participate in God's ongoing work of shaping souls with the same patient love we received.

Amazing Grace Challenge

This week, reflect on the "potter's hands" that have shaped your life—fathers, mentors, teachers, or spiritual guides who helped form your character. Consider how their influence continues to work through you today.

Look for one opportunity to be a potter's hand in someone else's life. It might be offering patient guidance to a grandchild, mentoring someone newer to your community, or simply demonstrating the same faithful presence that shaped you. Remember: the potter's wheel keeps turning, and now it's your turn to shape others with the love you received.

Today I witnessed Grace when:

The Sacred Dance

Paul and Norma Smith have been doing the Sacred Dance for 75 years. Photo Credit: daughter Joy Davis.

Above all, love each other deeply, because love covers over a multitude of sins. —1 Peter 4:8 (NIV)

A sacred dance unfolds in the early morning quiet of our retirement community. Loving spouses rise before dawn, moving with gentle purpose as they care for partners facing health challenges. These early hours are filled with small acts of devotion that sustain the person they promised to cherish decades ago—adjusting pillows, organizing medications, and preparing breakfast with the same care they once packed school lunches for their children.

For many couples, diagnoses like Parkinson's, Alzheimer's, or stroke have transformed their daily lives. Yet behind these physical changes remains the same wonderful person they fell in love with, the teacher whose eyes still light up when discussing former students, the parent whose face transforms at the sight of grandchildren, the gardener whose fingers instinctively reach to tend plants even when walking has become difficult, the veteran who salutes every flag he passes by.

Those wedding vows of "in sickness and in health" have taken on a profound meaning that young couples could never have imagined. Love in these twilight years doesn't ask for perfect circumstances or the energy of youth; it simply asks for presence, for showing up day after day with open hearts and willing hands.

Throughout our community, couples have established sacred rhythms that honor both struggle and resilience. Morning medications are shared with breakfast and gentle conversation. Therapy sessions are approached as team efforts, and quiet moments are spent gazing out the windows, where nature's beauty provides comfort and distraction from discomfort. Tasks that once took minutes might now require much longer, but they become celebrations of navigating life together.

Daily routines transform into moments of profound connection. Meals become opportunities to reminisce about adventures shared over decades—that first apartment, raising children, building careers, weathering storms together. Even medication management becomes infused with gratitude for the precious time these treatments provide and the blessing of having someone who cares enough to help.

The wisest caregivers have learned to protect their own well-being, understanding that martyrdom serves no one. The initial guilt of taking personal time gradually transforms into wisdom, recognizing that self-care sustains the capacity to give care. They accept help from children, friends, and community services, knowing that asking for support is not a weakness but wisdom.

Those outside this experience might see only challenges, perhaps even offering pity with well-meaning but misplaced sympathy. What they miss is the profound deepening of love that occurs through shared vulnerability. Each day provides new opportunities to show partners they matter, that they remain the same beautiful souls who first captured hearts decades ago, even when bodies fail and minds sometimes wander.

My neighbor Norma moves through her day of caregiving like a living prayer. You can see the appreciation flowing between these couples—a communion of souls rising above the challenges of aging bodies. In their weathered faces is the wisdom of those who have discovered that love's most significant expression sometimes comes not in the passion of romance but in the quiet dignity of daily care.

I think of Gracelyn and her fellow midshipmen, many of whom have grandparents demonstrating this same sacred dance of caregiving back home. While they're learning military discipline and leadership at the Academy, their grandparents are quietly teaching lessons about a different kind of service—the daily commitment to love someone through their most vulnerable seasons. These young men and women are witnessing, even from a distance, what faithful love looks like when tested by time and circumstance.

These caregiving couples in our community teach us that true love stories don't end with "happily ever after"; they continue with "faithfully ever after," written in the daily choices to honor the sacred trust of marriage when it matters most. They remind us that the deepest love isn't found in grand gestures or perfect moments, but in the steady commitment to dance together through every season, even when the steps become slower and the music grows softer.

In watching these couples, I see a reflection of God's own faithful love for us—patient, enduring, and present in our weakest moments. Their sacred dance becomes a living prayer, a testament to the truth that love, when rooted in commitment and nurtured by grace, only grows deeper with time.

Amazing Grace Challenge

Someday, we will either need a caregiver or be called upon to be one. If you are called to be a caregiver, thank God for the strength to serve in this holy work. Remember to take needed breaks for self-care. A visit with a neighbor, a moment for coffee, or time to rest—as you continue this journey of love. Your sacrifice is seen and honored, both by the one you serve and by the God who calls us to love deeply.

If you're not currently in a caregiving role, look for ways to support those who are. Offer to sit with their loved one for an hour, bring a meal, or listen when they need to share their heart. We're all part of this sacred dance of love and service.

Today I witnessed Grace when:

Home Is Where the Heart Is

Norm Tramba and Dana Donovan at Wilber, Nebraska airport. Photo Credit: Ron Ramsey.

For where your treasure is, there your heart will be also. —Matthew 6:21 (NIV)

As I celebrate our 50th wedding anniversary today, I reflect on what "home" truly means. Since leaving high school, I've lived in fifteen different places, but for the longest time, "home" was always our farmhouse south of Centerview, Kansas. I can still close my eyes and be transported there—the sweet scent of fresh-cut wheat in the summer breeze, the grand white barn standing proud against the endless blue sky, horses grazing contentedly in the pasture.

When my parents sold the homestead where Dad was born and raised, I was devastated. How could they leave behind the walls that echoed with decades of our laughter, the fields where we played hide-and-seek among the tall corn stalks, and the warm kitchen where Mom baked those delicious meals, especially her famous cherry pies that no one has ever been able to replicate?

But today, after sharing 50 years of life with Norm, I finally understand my parents' choice. I've now spent more years building a life with my husband than I ever did on that beloved farm. Gradually, almost imperceptibly, my definition of "home" has shifted from a place to a person.

It was meaningful to become the third generation in our family to marry on August 23rd, following in the footsteps of my parents, Carl and LeNora Donovan, and Dad's parents, James and Ethel Donovan. This legacy of love has taught me something precious: Mom and Dad eventually recognized that home had become wherever they were together.

How are we celebrating this golden milestone? Our first date was nothing fancy—just two young people sharing a pizza and endless conversation. So tonight, that's exactly where we're headed: out for pizza, coming full circle to where our journey began half a century ago.

I think of Gracelyn at the Naval Academy, learning her own lessons about what makes a place feel like home. For midshipmen, home becomes the shipmates who have your back during challenging training, the roommate who helps you prepare for inspections, and the study group that gets you through difficult exams. She's discovering that military families create home wherever they're stationed—that the Navy teaches you home isn't a zip code, it's the people who become your chosen family.

The Academy is preparing her for a life where "home" will constantly change. She'll serve on ships, live in different ports, and eventually make homes in places she's never imagined. But she's learning what Norm and I discovered over five decades: home is built not on geography, but on the relationships that anchor your heart.

Norm has shown me throughout our lives what unconditional love looks like. He has always been there to protect me, demonstrating a servant's heart through his care for me, our two sons, and their families. He has always provided what we needed, creating havens of safety wherever we lived. His quiet love was demonstrated through daily actions rather than grand gestures.

Even though I still have fond memories of that Kansas farm, I've learned the beautiful truth that home travels with you when it's built on love. Whether Grace finds herself stationed in Norfolk, San Diego, or halfway around the world, she'll carry with her the understanding that home is created by the people who choose to walk through life together.

Amazing Grace Challenge

This week, celebrate the people who have made life feel like "home" for you. Write a note or have a conversation with someone who has created that sense of belonging in your heart—whether it's a spouse, family member, or dear friend. Share specifically how their presence has been your safe harbor through life's seasons.

Remember that home isn't built on grand gestures, but on the daily choice to be each other's safe place in this world.

Today I witnessed Grace when:

Gone Fishin': Lessons from Rattlesnake Creek

♥

Donovan Tramba fishing in North Carolina. Photo Credit: Todd Tramba.

"I'm going out to fish," Simon Peter told them, and they said, "We'll go with you." So they went out and got into the boat, but that night they caught nothing.
—John 21:3 (NIV)

My Dad lived for those rare moments on the water. Whenever he could escape the endless demands of farm chores, he would gather us three kids like precious cargo and journey to Rattlesnake Creek to fish. The truth is, Dad rarely got his line wet. Instead, he spent those precious hours patiently untangling our fishing lines from low-hanging branches, stubborn bushes, and half-submerged logs in the creek bed.

One particularly memorable afternoon, after freeing my hook for what must have been the tenth time, his patience finally gave way to exasperation.

"Dandy," he said with a deep sigh that carried equal parts frustration and tenderness, "go up to the middle of the road and cast your line as far as you like. There's nothing up there to catch that hook on."

I scrambled eagerly up the creek bank, positioned myself squarely in the center of the dusty country road, squeezed my eyes shut tight, and cast with every ounce of strength my small arms could muster. When I opened my eyes, I watched in quiet horror as my red and white bobber completed its graceful arc directly into the telephone wire stretching above the road.

The shame of failure washed over me, but pride kept me silent. I let my pole hang suspended in the air, found a stick nearby, and began drawing patterns in the sand, pretending nothing was wrong. When Dad eventually made his way up the bank, his eyes followed my fishing line skyward. Without a word, he pulled his worn pocketknife from the front pocket of his overalls, cut the line with a single swift motion, tossed my pole into the bed of our pickup, and said, "Get in; we're heading home."

For years afterward, whenever our family drove down that same dirt road, I would crane my neck to search the telephone wire for my lost bobber. Then, I would turn around completely in my seat, pressing my face against the rear window, watching that spot until the distance swallowed it from view.

I often reflect on that afternoon and wonder about the infinite patience of our Heavenly Father as He untangles the complicated messes we create. He has undoubtedly had His hands full straightening out my tangled paths, but He never stops loving us, just as my earthly Daddy never stopped being patient with our fishing disasters.

This memory serves as a perfect metaphor for our lives. Sometimes, the things we cast out with such confidence end up tangled in places we never anticipated. We might believe we're concealing our mistakes, but our Heavenly Father sees everything. He knows precisely which telephone wires hold our bobbers, which dreams get caught mid-flight, and which hopes become suspended between heaven and earth.

I think about Gracelyn at the Naval Academy, where she's learning to cast her line into unfamiliar waters. Like those childhood fishing trips, some of her efforts will land perfectly in the clear stream, while others might get tangled in unexpected places. The Academy teaches midshipmen that leadership means learning from failed attempts, adjusting their aim, and casting again with renewed confidence.

When she faces setbacks—a difficult exam, a challenging training exercise, moments of doubt about her chosen path—I pray she'll remember that even tangled lines don't mean the fishing trip is over. Sometimes you need someone with experience to help cut you free so you can try again. The officers who mentor her are like my father at the creek—patiently untangling whatever gets caught, teaching through their actions rather than their words.

We tend to recall the tangles first, the times our lines caught, the moments Dad had to cut us loose, the shame of failure. But what about the fish we caught? The fun we had by the creek? The uncontrollable giggles when someone slipped and got soaked to the knees? Gracelyn will discover the same truth: the successes and joys of her Academy experience will far outweigh the temporary frustrations she may encounter.

I chose the cover of my memoir—a winding dirt road—because it perfectly captured my memories of Rattlesnake Creek and the journey to understanding God's plan. The title, Making Peace with the Pieces of My Life, reflects exactly what writing these stories has been for me: a healing journey where I began to recognize God's fingerprints on what I once thought were mere coincidences.

Like that long-ago bobber caught in the telephone wire, some experiences in our lives seem stuck in places we never expected. But God sees the whole picture—our tangled lines and our perfect casts, our failures and our successes—and He's writing a beautiful story through all of it.

Amazing Grace Challenge

This week, take time for your own "fishing trip" down memory lane. Focus on the "fish you landed"—moments of joy, success, or connection that you want to celebrate and remember more clearly, rather than dwelling on the lines that got tangled.

Like my father patiently untangling our fishing lines, practice extending grace to someone in your life who might be struggling with their own tangled situation. Offer help without judgment, just as God continues to lovingly work through our messes.

Today I witnessed Grace when:

Facing Fear: Lessons from a Dog

Norm and Dana Tramba with Daisy. Photo Credit: Jennifer McGaugh.

Be strong and courageous. Do not be afraid or terrified because of them, for the Lord your God goes with you; he will never leave you nor forsake you.
—Deuteronomy 31:6 (NIV)

When my friend Linda Harris had a medical emergency, I temporarily took in her Shih Tzu, Baron. Our dog Daisy was not happy about this new visitor in her territory. Although much smaller than Baron, Daisy was determined to protect her family and home, following me everywhere and staying alert to this perceived threat.

Watching Daisy's anxious behavior made me think about how we handle our own fears and uncertainties. Like my little dog, we often feel protective of our familiar routines and spaces, especially here in our retirement community, where we've worked hard to create a sense of security and belonging.

Just as Daisy couldn't understand my reassurances that Baron was only a temporary guest, we sometimes struggle to accept comfort when facing our own worries—concerns about our health, our independence, or our family members far away. Our minds can spiral into anxiety about worst-case scenarios, making us feel sick with worry or unable to sleep at night.

But Daisy also taught me something beautiful about trust and comfort. Despite her initial fears about Baron, she never stopped seeking my presence. At night, she would still snuggle under our bed, finding peace in being close to those she loved. During the day, she stayed near my feet, drawing comfort from familiar companionship even in the midst of her uncertainty.

I think about Gracelyn at the Naval Academy, learning to navigate her own form of unfamiliar territory. Like Daisy adapting to an unexpected houseguest, Grace is adjusting to life with roommates from different backgrounds, new routines, and the constant presence of people she's still getting to know.

The structured environment requires her to find comfort and security in new ways.

Until she went to the Academy, Gracelyn always had dogs in her life—companions who showed her unconditional love, ran with her, played with her, and slept beside her. They alerted her when strangers approached and provided a constant, reassuring presence. Now she's learning to find that same sense of security and belonging among her fellow midshipmen, building trust and camaraderie in a more complex social environment.

Both Daisy's situation and Gracelyn's Academy experience remind us that change often brings anxiety, even when the change ultimately serves our good. Daisy eventually learned that Baron wasn't a threat, just as Gracelyn is discovering that her new military family provides its own form of protection and support.

The news fills us with dangers and uncertainties—conflicts, natural disasters, and threats that make us worry about our children's and grandchildren's futures. Here in our retirement community, we often gather over coffee to discuss these concerns, sharing fears about loved ones serving in the military or living in uncertain times.

But just as Daisy never left my side despite her fears, God promises never to leave or forsake us. "Be strong and courageous. Do not be afraid or terrified because of them, for the Lord your God goes with you; he will never leave you nor forsake you." (Deuteronomy 31:6)

We can choose to focus on the troubles—the aches and pains of aging, the uncertainty of tomorrow, our worries about grandchildren far from home—or we can take heart that our Savior has already overcome anything this world can throw at us. Like Daisy finding comfort by staying close to those who love her, we can find peace by drawing near to God, even when circumstances feel unfamiliar or threatening.

Amazing Grace Challenge
This week, when anxiety begins to spiral, practice "staying close" like Daisy did with me. Instead of allowing your mind to race toward worst-case scenarios, consciously choose to draw near to God through prayer, scripture, or quiet reflection.

Consider reaching out to a fellow resident, family member, or friend when worries feel overwhelming. Sometimes comfort comes through the simple act of staying close to those who care about us, just as our pets instinctively seek our presence during uncertain times.

Today I witnessed Grace when:

The Joy Ride of Life

♥

Silver Dollar City, CC BY 2.0. Photo
Credit: Jeremy Thompson from Los Angeles,
California - Wikimedia Commons

*Forget the former things; do not dwell on the past. See,
I am doing a new thing.* —Isaiah 43:18-19a (NIV)

The wooden roller coaster creaked as it climbed the steep incline. Thirteen-year-old Elijah sat wide-eyed next to his grandfather, his knuckles white as he gripped the safety bar. Papa Norm, a retired acrobatic pilot who had danced with clouds and kissed the sky, placed his weathered hand over his grandson's trembling one.

"Come on. This is fun!" Norm's eyes twinkled with childlike wonder.

I watched from below as their car disappeared over the first peak of the Outlaw Run—the world's fastest wooden roller coaster with three heart-stopping loops. The screams that followed told me they had begun their plunge into the unknown.

What struck me most was Elijah's transformation. What changed for him wasn't the roller coaster itself—the loops were just as steep, the drops just as dramatic. Through his grandfather's encouragement and steady presence, fear gave way to anticipation. The unknown became an adventure rather than a threat.

This scene perfectly captures what I see happening across generations in our lives. In our retirement community, we face our own set of fears—health concerns, loss of independence, the great unknown that lies beyond this life. Yet we're learning that we don't ride alone. Sometimes we're the frightened child needing reassurance; other times we're the experienced pilot offering a steady hand to others.

I think of Gracelyn at the Naval Academy, strapped into her own version of the Outlaw Run. Plebe Summer was her steep climb—every day bringing new challenges, rigorous training, and discipline that would terrify most young people. But like

Elijah with his grandfather, she's surrounded by experienced guides who've ridden this ride before. Her company officers and upperclassmen become her "Papa Norms," placing steady hands over her trembling ones and saying, "Come on, this is part of the adventure."

The Academy teaches midshipmen that courage isn't the absence of fear—it's learning to trust your training, your teammates, and something greater than yourself when facing the unknown. Every drill, every formation, every challenge is designed to transform that initial white-knuckled terror into the confidence that comes from being part of something larger.

Here in our golden years, we're discovering the same truth. The question isn't whether there will be dips and loops ahead—there surely will be. The question is whether we'll face them with fear or faith, isolation or community. Isaiah reminds us: "See, I am doing a new thing!" Even in our twilight years, God continues to write new chapters of our story.

Just as Norm's presence transformed Elijah's terror into excitement, our Heavenly Father walks beside us through every twist and turn. And like experienced pilots, we can offer our own steady hands to those just beginning their ride—whether it's a new resident adjusting to community life, a grandchild facing their own challenges, or a fellow traveler navigating unexpected health concerns.

The beautiful truth is that every generation needs both the wisdom of experience and the courage to embrace what's new. Elijah needs Papa Norm's reassurance, Grace needs her Academy mentors, and we need each other as we navigate the adventures still ahead.

When I pause to consider what frightens me today—perhaps trying a new activity, reaching out to someone I don't know well, or facing a medical appointment—I imagine placing my hand in the hand of my Heavenly Father. Then I take a deep breath and whisper to myself, "Come on, this will be fun!" and step forward into that challenge with the trust of a child and the wisdom of well-lived years.

Amazing Grace Challenge

This week, be someone's "Papa Norm." Find a person in your community who might be facing their own "roller coaster moment"—perhaps someone new, dealing with a health challenge, or hesitant about joining activities. Offer to be their steady hand and encouraging voice, helping them see adventure where they might only see threat.

Today I witnessed Grace when:

Where Do You Spend Your Time?

Gracelyn. Photo Credit: Gracelyn's friend at NAPS.

Therefore do not worry about tomorrow, for tomorrow will worry about itself. Each day has enough trouble of its own. —Adapted from Matthew 6:25-34 (NIV)

While reading my 2017 journal, I encountered a question from William P. Young's novel *The Shack* that stopped me cold: "Where do you spend most of your time in your mind—in the present, in the past, or in the future?"

I made a startling discovery: I spend very little time in the present moment. Instead, my mental energy is divided between two demanding territories: the past and the future.

Much of my mental energy goes toward looking backward—writing memoirs, reading old journals, gazing into life's rear-view mirror, trying to make sense of the journey I've traveled. The remaining hours are spent worrying about what lies ahead: our troubled world, whether my children will manage financially, and whether my grandchildren will develop the resilience needed for their futures.

Yesterday morning, I caught myself doing exactly this. While sitting on our patio with my coffee, instead of enjoying the cool breeze and morning light, my mind was racing between memories of my childhood farm and anxieties about Grace's upcoming military assignments. I completely missed the cardinal that landed just three feet away—Norm had to point it out twice before I noticed.

In *The Shack*, God tells Mack: "When I dwell with you, I do so in the present. Not the past, although much can be learned by looking back, but only for a visit, not an extended stay." The passage continued: "Do you realize that your imagination of the future, which is almost always dictated by fear, rarely pictures me there with you?"

This hit me hard. When I envision potential challenges my family might face or imagine difficulties that could arise in our world, I picture them navigating these trials alone. I forget to include God's presence in these imagined scenarios.

I think of Gracelyn at the Naval Academy, where the structured discipline naturally teaches present-moment living. During her first six weeks without phones or watches, she had no choice but to focus entirely on the immediate task at hand—whether it was folding uniforms to precise specifications, memorizing rates and recognition, or keeping up during grueling physical training.

The Academy's demanding schedule forces midshipmen to be fully present because distraction can mean failure. When she's standing at attention during inspection, her mind can't wander to next week's exam or last month's family gathering. She must be completely present to the officer examining her uniform, the posture of her shoulders, the expression on her face.

This is what I'm still learning in my golden years—how to be fully present in each moment rather than scattered across time. Here in our retirement community, I'm discovering that present-moment living involves really listening when my neighbor shares about her grandchildren, rather than mentally planning my response. It means noticing the way afternoon light falls across our dining room, appreciating the skill in the kitchen staff's meal preparation, and finding genuine interest in the stories my tablemates tell.

The present moment is where life actually happens—where I taste my morning coffee, hear Norm in his office, and feel gratitude for our comfortable home. It's where love is experienced, beauty is noticed, and I sense God's presence more clearly than in any imagined future scenario or nostalgic memory.

This truth is beautifully captured in Helen Hauncoatt's poem that has become a touchstone for me:

MY NAME IS I AM by Helen Hauncoatt

I was regretting the past
and fearing the future.

Suddenly, my Lord was speaking:
"My name is I Am."

He paused. I waited. He continued.

"When you live in the past
with its mistakes and regrets, it is hard.

I am not there.

My name is not I WAS.

When you live in the future,
with its problems and fears, it is hard.

I am not there.

My name is not I WILL BE.

When you live in this moment, it is not hard.

I am here.

My name is I AM."

Learning to live in the present doesn't mean ignoring legitimate concerns or failing to make reasonable preparations. It means recognizing which worries require prudent action and which ones steal our peace without serving any useful purpose.

Most importantly, it means trusting that whatever comes, we won't face it alone.

Amazing Grace Challenge

This week, practice "present moment check-ins" three times daily. Set gentle reminders to pause and notice: What do I see right now? What do I hear? What am I grateful for in this exact moment? When your mind starts racing toward past regrets or future fears, gently redirect it to something immediate and tangible—the feeling of your feet on the ground, the sound of your breathing, or the view from your window.

Today I witnessed Grace when:

September 11th -
The Day Everything
Changed

The Twin Towers, NYC. Photo Credit: Wikimedia Commons.

Be very careful, then, how you live—not as unwise
but as wise, making the most of every opportunity.
—Ephesians 5:15-16 (NIV)

At 8:45 a.m. on September 11th, 2001, I was conducting an employee workshop at the Robert S. Dole Veterans Administration Medical Center in Wichita when a man rushed in and turned on the television. We watched in disbelief as the first plane hit the World Trade Center's north tower, then witnessed the horror of the second plane striking the south tower. Both towers collapsing into deadly rubble is an image I can never erase from my mind.

I immediately rushed to the waiting rooms to be with our Veterans. All day, they came to the VA—reliving wars they had fought, battles they had survived. They needed to be with people who understood the weight of service and sacrifice.

The next day, I joined Veterans and fellow employees on the street in front of the VA, proudly waving our flag as rush-hour traffic drove by, horns honking in solidarity. We wanted the world to know that nothing, not even this unthinkable tragedy, could keep us from serving our Veterans.

That day taught me that tomorrow isn't promised. Watching the sudden loss of nearly 3,000 innocent lives showed me what truly mattered: the precious, irreplaceable connections we have with the people we love. In December 2001, while rescue workers were still digging through rubble in New York, I planned a family reunion with relatives I hadn't seen in years.

Now, more than two decades later, I think about Gracelyn at the Naval Academy, learning to embody "Peace through Strength." She's training in cyber warfare, global strategy, and crisis response—skills that emerged from hard lessons learned on 9/11. Her generation of naval officers will serve in a world forever changed by that September morning, where threats can come from hijacked airplanes, computer networks, or lone actors inspired by extremist ideologies.

The Academy is preparing her not just to fight wars, but to prevent them through deterrence, diplomacy, and the kind of military readiness that makes potential enemies think twice. She's part of a new generation who understand viscerally that freedom isn't free—a lesson written in the ashes of 9/11 and reinforced through every training exercise, every leadership challenge, and every oath of service.

At our retirement community dining hall, we eat alongside former nurses, doctors, governors, teachers, business leaders, and Veterans—including a former POW. When Gracelyn dines with us, something magical happens. Stories flow freely between generations as our Veterans share tales of service that help her understand the weight of her commitment, while she brings fresh Academy perspectives that remind us why we served.

Norm and I visited the Flight 93 Memorial in Pennsylvania, where we listened to recordings of passengers' final phone calls—voices saying "I love you" in what they knew might be their last moments. Those words, spoken facing unimaginable terror, carry power that transcends time.

Every time I tell Gracelyn "I love you," I think about those passengers and the thousands of final messages that were never sent that day. Whatever challenges Grace faces in her naval career, she carries with her the love of family and the wisdom of Veterans who've walked this path before her.

The lessons of 9/11 aren't just about remembering tragedy—they're about understanding that life can change in an instant, that ordinary people become heroes when circumstances demand it, and that love expressed clearly and often is our greatest defense against despair.

Gracelyn is preparing to defend freedoms we discovered could be threatened in ways we never imagined. But she's also inheriting the resilience, unity, and unwavering commitment to each other that emerged from that day's ashes.

Amazing Grace Challenge

It's never too late or too early to say what needs to be said. Take time today to call your family and tell them you love them. Share your stories with younger generations—they need to hear about events that shaped our world and values that sustained us. Listen to their stories too, as they share events currently shaping their lives.

Remember, God is with us in every struggle. He is our safe place, and He loves you.

Today I witnessed Grace when:

Unmasking and Finding Our True Selves

♥

Gracelyn at Naval Academy during Plebe summer.
Photo Credit: Thorton Studios, Annapolis, MD.

The Lord does not look at the things people look at.
People look at the outward appearance, but the Lord
looks at the heart. —1 Samuel 16:7 (NIV)

The word "Halloween" paints a vivid picture of autumn leaves, plump pumpkins, and sticky caramel apples. My cherished memories take me back to Kansas in the early 1950s—fields of rustling cornstalks, golden mums, and my mother lovingly crafting our Halloween costumes by hand.

Around 1953, my sister Dee wore an elaborate pig costume designed with chicken wire and pillows. "Come on, Porky!" my brother Dennis and I would tease as we held her hands, helping her waddle up neighbors' sidewalks to trick-or-treat. We were determined not to let her slip out of her "pig skin" as she collected her treats.

In other years, white sheets transformed us into friendly ghosts like Casper. I once dressed as Robin Hood, sporting green leotards and a pointed hat adorned with a carefully dyed red chicken feather, which my mother had made. Dennis preferred his black mask, which made him look like the Lone Ranger as he galloped through the neighborhood.

One particularly memorable Halloween, Mom and Dad joined the festivities in matching clown costumes Mom had sewn. We visited families throughout our farm community—people we knew personally. The neighbors' challenge was to guess who was hiding beneath each mask. To everyone's amusement, not a single farmer could identify my parents!

That night taught me something unexpected: sometimes wearing a costume actually reveals something true about us. My parents, usually so serious and hardworking, showed their playful, joyful sides through those clown outfits. The "disguise" allowed their lighter spirits to emerge in ways that their everyday roles as responsible farmers rarely permitted.

This memory prompts me to reflect on the various roles we play throughout our lives, not false masks, but the authentic parts of ourselves that emerge in different seasons and situations. During my working years, I wore the "costume" of a professional nurse, which wasn't a pretense but rather one facet of who I am: someone who cares deeply about helping others heal. At church, I wore the "costume" of a community member, expressing my faith through service and fellowship.

Now in retirement, I'm discovering which costumes I can finally set aside, and which ones were actually part of my true self all along. The pressure to appear perpetually busy has been replaced by the freedom to move at my own pace. The need to have all the answers has given way to the wisdom of admitting what I don't know.

I think of Gracelyn at the Naval Academy, where she's learning to balance different aspects of her identity. She's the same person who grew up loving her dogs and family dinners, but she's also developing into a disciplined military officer. The Academy isn't asking her to become someone else; it is helping her discover strengths and capabilities she may not have known she possessed. Like my parents in their clown costumes, the military "uniform" of discipline and service may be revealing parts of her character that were always there, waiting for the right circumstances to emerge.

The Academy's honor code demands authenticity: "Midshipmen are persons of integrity. We stand for that which is right." This isn't about removing masks; it's about ensuring that all the roles you play align with your core values. Grace is learning that true leadership requires being the same person in private as you are in public, whether you're in uniform or civilian clothes.

Here in our retirement community, I'm experiencing a similar kind of authenticity. There's less energy for pretense and more appreciation for genuine connection. When someone asks how I'm doing, I'm more likely to give an honest answer—not to complain, but to allow real relationships to form. This isn't about removing a mask; it's about having the freedom to be fully myself without apology.

As I've matured, I've realized that the goal isn't to strip away all our various roles and responsibilities, but to ensure they all spring from the same authentic source. Like my parents' clown costumes that revealed their hidden playfulness, each season of our lives can uncover different aspects of who God created us to be.

Amazing Grace Challenge

This week, reflect on which aspects of your personality have emerged more fully since entering retirement. Perhaps you've discovered a more patient side, a creative spirit, or a deeper capacity for friendship. Embrace these qualities as gifts that have been waiting for the right season to bloom.

Consider sharing one authentic part of yourself with someone in your community—a hobby you've always loved, a story from your past that has shaped you, or a dream you're still pursuing. Let others see the full, genuine person you've become. Remove your mask.

Today I witnessed Grace when:

The Ice Storm: A Lesson in Balance

Ice Storm at Heritage Hills in Oklahoma City. Photo Credit: Todd Tramba.

He caused the storm to be still, so that the waves of the
sea were hushed. —Psalm 10:29 (NIV)

When Norm and I moved from sunny Arizona to our new retirement community in Edmond, Oklahoma, we barely had time to unpack before nature taught us a powerful lesson. Just two weeks after settling in, I looked out my window to discover our landscape had transformed overnight. Tree branches—still heavy with autumn leaves—bent and snapped under the weight of ice. The scene was breathtaking yet destructive: snow clinging to leaves that hadn't yet fallen, creating a burden too great for branches never designed to carry such loads.

Our trees were not made to carry this extra weight. Neither are we.

This frozen spectacle became a mirror of my own life. How often had I taken on more commitments than I could handle? My calendar was perpetually overflowing with promises I'd made because I couldn't bring myself to say that simple yet powerful word: "No." Some friends don't understand that my "Happy Place" is simply being home with Norm, in my office, writing.

As I watched this natural lesson unfold outside my window, I thought of Gracelyn's endless energy at the Naval Academy—always embracing new challenges, leading organizations, starring in drama productions, designing and building sets with her father, and rising two hours early for runs. Her schedule mirrors what mine once looked like, packed with worthy activities that nonetheless threatened to overwhelm.

I recognized the same pattern in myself when we first arrived here—not rising at dawn to run, but diving into water aerobics daily, attending countless activities, and teaching memoir classes. The commitments accumulated like ice on branches, each one seemingly manageable until their combined weight became too much to bear.

The Academy's rigorous demands will teach Gracelyn what took me decades to learn—that saying "yes" to everything eventually means saying "no" to what matters most. I hope she discovers sooner than I did that pausing to evaluate what we truly want to pursue isn't giving up, it's growing wise. How do you discover balance when you're naturally driven to excel?

Every choice to take on new commitments has consequences—but so does the choice to let them go. When I finally decided to release some activities that brought more stress than joy, I felt lighter, deeply relieved, and peaceful. Why carry the weight of obligations that drain you when freedom awaits after a simple "no"?

Start by examining your calendar honestly. Look at each entry and ask: Does this task energize me or deplete me? If you feel no joy—only obligation or worry—perhaps it's time to release that commitment before it breaks under the strain.

The secret to a fulfilling life isn't cramming every moment with activity but instead investing yourself fully in what truly matters. Like those Oklahoma trees after the ice melted, we can regain our natural strength and grace when we release what we were never meant to carry.

Let's shake off the accumulated burdens from our branches and rediscover our authentic rhythm. Choose with intention. Focus on what aligns with your deepest values. Find the courage to say no to what doesn't serve your truest purpose.

Like those trees standing tall and unburdened after the spring thaw, we too can flourish when we're no longer weighted down by commitments that were never ours to carry. In letting go, we discover not emptiness, but the spaciousness to grow into who we were always meant to be.

Amazing Grace Challenge

Your calendar reflects your life choices—take control of it with gentle firmness. Practice declining invitations that don't align with your values and energy. Select activities that nourish your spirit and bring genuine joy. Remember, you have the power to create the life that feels authentically yours.

Today I witnessed Grace when:

The Gift of Neighboring

♥

Shirlee Smith, Lynn Payne, Linda Anderson, and Dana Tramba
at Inspirations Tea Room in Edmond, OK.

Do not forget to show hospitality to strangers, for by so doing some people have shown hospitality to angels without knowing it. —Hebrews 13:2 (NIV)

Right here in our community, we have neighbors living just steps away—sometimes right next door. Behind each door lies potential for love, warmth, wisdom, and happiness. What we must do is look for the connection and be willing to make the first move.

Drop in to see a neighbor. There's already a foundation—you share this place, this chapter of life. That's a connection enough to start with.

I think of our granddaughter Gracelyn, who is also learning the art of neighboring in her own unique environment. At the Naval Academy, midshipmen rotate roommates every few months, but this isn't just about making friends—it's about building the kind of trust that could one day save lives. When your roommate might become your shipmate, navigating dangerous waters or making split-second decisions in a crisis, neighboring takes on life-and-death significance.

The Academy teaches that looking out for your neighbor isn't just kindness—it's duty. Their honor code demands it: "Midshipmen do not lie, cheat, steal, or tolerate those who do." But there's an unwritten code just as powerful: you watch your roommate's back, you help them succeed, and you never let a classmate fall behind without offering a hand. Gracelyn is learning that in military life, your neighbor's failure can become everyone's failure, and your neighbor's strength becomes everyone's strength.

A small display of kindness can have life-changing consequences. Saying hello or offering thanks creates an easy bridge between two human beings. Today, start with the people who cross your path most often: our neighbors, the grocery clerks, the maintenance staff, the delivery drivers. Everyone who becomes part of our everyday rhythm deserves recognition and connection.

While Gracelyn practices neighboring with the intensity of military discipline, we in retirement have discovered neighboring as a gentle art. We have what she doesn't yet possess: time. Time to notice when our neighbor hasn't picked up her mail in two days. Time to sit with a widower when he shares memories of his late wife. Time to really listen when someone needs to talk through their worries about adult children or health concerns.

Think of each person as a fellow traveler on this life journey. How do you see the world around you? Do you view it as cold, random, and disconnected? Or do you see it as rich with possibilities—full of relationships waiting to unfold and opportunities to love, share, and grow together?

Sometimes we meet someone and wonder: Why is this person suddenly in my life? What beautiful connection might this be?

I've learned to call these moments "God-incidences" rather than coincidences. Perhaps the person struggling with loneliness was placed next door to someone who understands. Maybe the neighbor with gardening expertise lives beside someone yearning to grow things. Possibly the retired teacher lives across from someone who needs patient encouragement.

Both Gracelyn and I are discovering the same truth in different settings: the people placed in our path aren't accidents. At the Academy, she might room with someone whose family's military tradition helps her understand the importance of service, or whose engineering skills complement her leadership abilities. Here in our retirement community, I might find myself at dinner with a former nurse who understands the challenges of healthcare, or a retired teacher who shares my love of writing.

The answer is often more straightforward than we think. Perhaps we're meant to discover that the richest treasures aren't hidden in distant places—they're living right next door, waiting for us to knock.

Whether you're twenty-one and learning to trust your life to your shipmate, or in your golden years with time to see and care for those around you, the principle remains: neighboring is both an art and a calling. It requires courage to reach out, wisdom to listen well, and faith that the connections we make might be precisely what God intended.

Amazing Grace Challenge

Whose door do you need to knock on today? Your next meaningful friendship might be living just steps away, waiting for your simple "hello" to unlock a treasure trove of connection. Whether it's checking on a quiet neighbor or offering encouragement to someone struggling, remember that your small act of neighborliness might be the very gift someone needs today.

Today I witnessed Grace when:

God Tweets

♥

"God is Calling." Photo Credit: Wikimedia Commons.

My sheep near my voice, and I know them, and they
follow me. —John 10:27 (NIV)

We live in an age of instant communication, where messages flash across screens in rapid succession. In this era of constant connectivity, I found myself wondering: What if God communicated with us the way we now communicate with each other? What would divine messages look like if they arrived as short, direct notifications tailored to our digital attention spans?

The thought intrigued me as I watched Gracelyn and her generation navigate their world through screens— always receiving messages. Whether she's facing the rigorous challenges of military academy life or I'm adjusting to retirement community living, we both need guidance, comfort, and a sense of divine connection that transcends our circumstances.

So, I imagined opening my phone and finding these divine notifications waiting—gentle messages from the One who knows my heart better than I know it myself. What might these heavenly reminders look like?

"You forgot to start your morning with Me. Pause. Breathe. Remember who guides your day." How often I rush into my morning routine without that quiet moment of connection, forgetting that each day begins best in His presence.

"Have you nourished your soul with My Word today? The Bible isn't just a book—it's your lifeline." In our information-saturated world, it's easy to fill our minds with news and social media while neglecting the words that truly feed our spirits.

"Don't pass judgment until you have walked in another's shoes. Compassion is the language of love." This divine reminder challenges me daily, especially in our retirement community, where different personalities and perspectives sometimes clash.

"Is endless scrolling the best way to use your precious time? Each moment is a gift. Invest wisely." I picture God gently nudging us away from mindless digital consumption toward more meaningful pursuits.

"Call your neighbor who lives alone. Connection heals. Loneliness hurts." How many opportunities for ministry pass by simply because we're too busy or distracted to notice who needs a kind word or listening ear?

"New neighbors have arrived. It's time to welcome them. Hospitality opens hearts." Whether it's newcomers to our retirement community or Gracelyn meeting new classmates at the Academy, welcoming others creates bonds that last lifetimes.

"Don't worry about your loved ones—I am with them right now. My protection transcends understanding." This message speaks directly to my grandmother's heart as I pray for Gracelyn's safety and success in her military training.

Other divine messages might include reminders about road grace—slowing down to let cars merge, showing kindness even in traffic. Or gentle nudges to pray for the homeless person on the corner, to be still and find peace in silence, to put away our phones and engage in real conversation, to take walks and notice the beauty of creation around us.

These imagined divine messages speak to both the grandmother settling into retirement and the granddaughter facing military challenges. At the Naval Academy, Gracelyn may especially need reminders about not judging others, finding moments of stillness amid intense schedules, and remembering that God's protection extends beyond human understanding.

In our retirement community, these gentle nudges encourage us to engage more deeply with our neighbors, use our time more intentionally, and cultivate a greater awareness of those who need our prayers and presence.

Whether facing the stress of military training or the adjustments of retirement living, we all need these divine notifications toward what truly matters: connection with God, compassion for others, and mindful presence in each moment we're given.

Amazing Grace Challenge

God is all-seeing, all-knowing, all-powerful, and everywhere present with us. In a world of endless notifications, His message remains constant: You are loved. You are seen. You matter. What is God tweeting to you today? Are you listening?

Today I witnessed Grace when:

Childhood Chores: A Lesson in Faith and Patience

♥

A child holding eggs. Photo Credit: Wikimedia Commons.

So do not fear, for I am with you; do not be dismayed, for I am your God. I will strengthen you and help you; I will uphold you with my righteous right hand. —Isaiah 41:10 (NIV)

Some of life's most profound lessons come wrapped in the most ordinary moments. For me, one of those moments involved a dented tin bucket, a terrified six-year-old, and a father's gentle hands showing me how God works in our lives.

Around 1953, my daily chore was gathering eggs from our family's chicken coop. I carried a cream-colored, battle-scarred tin bucket that bore the evidence of my brothers' target practice—Daisy BB Gun holes scattered across its surface like tiny windows letting in slivers of sunlight.

Getting into the chicken house required a small adventure in itself. Dad had nailed a waist-high board across the entrance to keep our sheep from wandering in and devouring the chicken feed. At six years old, I had to crawl over this barrier every morning, bucket in hand, preparing myself for what lay ahead.

The chickens nested in a row of wooden boxes; each covered with gunny sack curtains that provided a shadowy privacy I found unsettling. But what I truly dreaded were the setting hens—those fierce, brooding mothers who viewed my small hands as threats to their precious eggs. They would peck relentlessly and refuse to budge from their nests, no matter how much I pleaded or tried to coax them away.

Dad always seemed to know when I was struggling. He would appear in the doorway of the chicken house and say with infinite patience, "This is how you do it, Dandy." I would watch in amazement as his large, tanned, work-scarred hands moved without hesitation toward the most aggressive hen. While she pecked furiously at his fingers, he would calmly reach beneath her, gather three eggs at once, and gently place them in my bucket—all without so much as a flinch.

One morning, after successfully gathering eggs from half the nests, I reached confidently into what I thought was an empty, dark corner nest. Instead of the familiar smooth coolness of an eggshell, I felt movement—and suddenly a giant grey rat leaped out, startling me so completely that I screamed and bolted toward the door.

In my panic, I forgot about Dad's barrier board. My legs caught on it, sending me tumbling to the gravel outside. My precious bucket flew from my hands, and I watched in horror as every single egg I'd carefully collected smashed on the ground around me. Adding insult to injury, I skinned my knee in the fall, and there I sat in the midst of my disaster, crying amid the broken shells and scattered straw.

Then I felt Daddy's strong arms lifting me up. He didn't scold me for the mess or lecture me about being more careful. Instead, he listened patiently as I sobbed out my story about the terrifying rat, my ruined eggs, and my throbbing knee. Together, we cleaned up the sticky mess of broken shells and egg whites. He carefully applied Mercurochrome to my scraped knee—that bright red antiseptic that stung initially but somehow made everything feel better.

Most importantly, he took my small hand in his large one, and together we finished my chores. He helped me gather a fresh bucket of eggs, standing beside me as I tentatively reached into each nest, his presence giving me the courage to continue.

That night, I prayed with the fervent desperation that only a six-year-old can muster: "Please, God, let me never have to gather eggs again."

Years passed. I continued my morning ritual with the dented bucket, gradually growing more comfortable with the setting hens and constantly checking dark corners carefully for unwanted surprises. I learned to navigate the barrier board with ease, and eventually, my father's patient lessons helped me become proficient at this childhood responsibility.

Then, ten years later, I graduated from high school and left home for college. God had answered my prayer—just not on my six-year-old timeline. I never had to gather eggs again.

Looking back now, I realize my daddy was unknowingly modeling how our Heavenly Father works in our lives. Just as Dad always knew when I was struggling in that chicken coop, God always knows what's happening in our hearts. Like my earthly father, He is patient in teaching us, gentle in listening to our fears, faithful in healing our pain, and always ready to embrace us when we fall.

Most importantly, He walks hand in hand with us through our challenges, giving us the strength and courage to face whatever "rats" might jump out of the dark corners of our lives. And just as my father taught me, our Heavenly Father always answers our prayers—but in His perfect timing, not ours.

The wisdom of teaching children responsibility through chores transcends generations. Just as my parents assigned age-appropriate tasks that built character, I've watched Gracelyn's parents do the same. While she didn't have eggs to gather, she had dogs to feed, trash and recycling to manage, and dishes to load—habits that create a foundation for lifelong responsibility. Now at the Naval Academy, she's learning that individual duties serve something greater than herself, contributing to the well-being of her entire company while developing the discipline and organizational skills that will serve her throughout her military career.

Whether it's a frightened six-year-old learning gentleness with setting hens or a midshipman discovering that careful attention to small duties prepares her for life-and-death responsibilities, the truth remains constant: God uses ordinary moments to shape extraordinary character. Here in our retirement community, I witness this same principle as neighbors find new purpose in mentoring newcomers and serving others, proving that no matter our age, He continues to use our daily experiences to refine our hearts.

Amazing Grace Challenge

As we reflect on our long lives, we can often see how prayers we thought went unanswered were answered in ways we couldn't have imagined. Think about the prayers you prayed years ago that seemed to take forever to be answered.

Can you see now how God's timing was perfect, even when it didn't match your own? Take a moment today to thank Him for the answered prayers, especially those that took decades to unfold.

Today I witnessed Grace when:

The Power of a Letter

♥

Dana Tramba writes in her notebook. Photo Credit: Gracelyn Tramba.

Therefore encourage one another and build each other up, just as in fact you are doing. —1 Thessalonians 5:11 (NIV)

Sometimes the most profound gifts come wrapped in the simplest gestures. For me, that gift was a letter—one that bridged forty years of silence and rekindled a friendship that had shaped my life in ways I was only beginning to understand.

In 1975, I worked alongside Beverly Burrell as a nurse at St. Luke's Hospital in Wellington, Kansas. At the time, I was navigating the aftermath of a difficult divorce, struggling through what felt like one of the darkest seasons of my life. Without realizing it, Beverly became a turning point in my life. Through her quiet example, she taught me how to prioritize God and family—a lesson that would resonate long after our paths diverged.

Life moved forward, as it does. I remarried, had children, and gradually transformed into what I now recognize as a "busy Martha." Work consumed more of my time, and providing material things for our two sons became my driving focus. The spiritual grounding Beverly had modeled seemed to fade into the background of my increasingly hectic life.

It wasn't until after retirement, forty years later, that I finally felt I had developed what I call the "Spirit of Mary"—that centered, reflective approach to life that prioritizes relationships and faith over endless activity. In this new season of clarity, I felt compelled to reach out to Beverly, to thank her for the impact she'd had during that crucial time in my young adult life.

So I wrote her a letter.

Finding the right words after forty years felt daunting. How do you tell someone they changed your life when they probably don't even remember the moments that mattered most? I struggled with whether my gratitude would seem genuine or merely sentimental after so much time had passed.

When we finally spoke, Beverly told me something that moved me deeply: she had kept that letter in her Bible. Those words I had worried over, wondering if they would matter after so many years, had become precious enough to preserve alongside Scripture.

We renewed our friendship and now talk every few weeks. Our roles have beautifully reversed—now I find myself offering encouragement to Beverly as she has transitioned into assisted living. It seems that God brought us back together for this new season, allowing us to support each other through the unique challenges and blessings of our later years.

This experience has shown me something I'm trying to pass on to Gracelyn through my own letters during Plebe summer at the Naval Academy. Just as Beverly's influence shaped me during a crucial season, Gracelyn is discovering mentors and friendships that will guide her through her military training and beyond. The difference is that I'm encouraging her not to wait forty years to express her gratitude.

I write to her regularly, knowing that the Academy's demanding schedule makes phone calls difficult. My letters aren't just updates—they're attempts to bridge our different worlds, to let her know that someone is thinking of her during the challenging moments when self-doubt creeps in or homesickness feels overwhelming. When she's feeling isolated during the rigorous demands of military training, I want her to have tangible reminders that she's loved and supported.

The Academy teaches midshipmen about the importance of maintaining connections with family and mentors throughout their careers. Unlike my forty-year gap with Beverly, Gracelyn is learning early that relationships require intentional cultivation, even across distance and demanding schedules. The letters I write to her now will hopefully inspire her to maintain these precious connections throughout her life.

Our retirement community has taught me that we're all part of an interconnected cycle of seasons. Some residents are in their active, independent phase, while others, like Beverly, are transitioning to a greater level of care. We support each other across these different seasons, understanding that today's helper may be tomorrow's recipient of care.

As I reflect on this unexpected gift of renewed friendship, I'm reminded that it's never too late to reach out, express gratitude, or acknowledge the ways someone has shaped your journey. In our retirement years, we have the luxury of perspective—we can see the patterns and influences that may have been invisible in the rush of earlier decades.

The letter that reconnected Beverly and me wasn't just about the past—it opened the door to a new season of mutual support and care. Sometimes the most healing thing we can do is acknowledge the gifts we've received, and sometimes, if we're fortunate, we discover those gifts can be renewed and shared all over again.

Amazing Grace Challenge

Who comes to mind when you think about the different seasons of your life? Is there someone who appeared when you needed them most, offering guidance, kindness, or simply their presence during a difficult time?

Write a letter to them. Express your gratitude for their impact, share how their influence shaped you, and let them know they mattered. If they are no longer living, write the letter anyway and keep it somewhere meaningful. Maybe in your Bible. Don't wait forty years—reach out today.

Today I witnessed Grace when:

Faith Under Pressure: Learning to Lead When You Feel Unqualified

Gracelyn takes a selfie at NAPS.

I can do all things through Christ who strengthens me. —Philippians 4:13 (NIV)

The phone call came that changed the trajectory of my nursing career. The Phoenix Carl T Hayden VA wanted me to design and manage their new call center—a role that would require supervising staff, managing budgets, and creating systems from scratch. My first thought wasn't excitement; it was panic. I'd been a bedside nurse for years, caring for patients one at a time. Now they wanted me to manage people and processes I'd never handled before.

"I've worked in call centers; however, I don't know anything about running a call center," I told the administrator during our meeting.

"That's exactly why we want you," she replied. "You'll figure it out."

Standing in the empty office space that would become our call center, I felt completely unqualified for the task ahead. I had nursing skills, not management experience. I understood patient care, not personnel supervision. Yet something deep inside whispered that this was where God wanted me, even if I couldn't see how I'd succeed.

Those first weeks were humbling in ways I hadn't expected. I had to write job descriptions for positions and learn the intricacies of call center operations while simultaneously explaining them to others. Most challenging of all, I had to project confidence I didn't feel while building a team that would depend on my leadership.

The hardest part was conducting performance evaluations for staff, as I was still learning what good performance looked like, counseling employees through difficult situations, and having those uncomfortable conversations when standards weren't being met. Each evaluation I wrote felt like I was learning as much about leadership as the person I was assessing.

During those months of building the call center from the ground up, I found myself clinging to Philippians 4:13: "I can do all things through Christ who strengthens me." It became my daily reminder that my adequacy didn't come from my experience or expertise, but from God's strength working through my willingness to try.

I think about Gracelyn now at the Naval Academy, facing her own moments of feeling unqualified for what's being asked of her. Whether it's leading her company when she's still learning the basics herself, or standing for inspection knowing she might not meet every standard, she's discovering what I learned at the VA: competence isn't a prerequisite for accepting responsibility—it's something you develop through the courage to begin.

The Academy is teaching her what the call center experience taught me: that the people who advance aren't necessarily those who start with the most knowledge, but those who are willing to embrace challenges that stretch them beyond their comfort zones. She's learning to say "I can do it" when opportunities arise and "I need help" when wisdom requires it, understanding that both responses take courage.

Just as I had to master juggling competing priorities—managing staff schedules, handling patient complaints, coordinating with different departments—Gracelyn is learning to balance academic demands, military training, and leadership responsibilities. Both of us discovered that success comes not from having all the answers, but from being willing to figure things out as you go.

One lesson from those VA days, in particular, applies to her military training: I learned that you cannot become a leader if you cannot follow. Before I could effectively supervise others, I had to learn to work within the VA's complex system, understanding how my call center fit into the larger mission of serving veterans. Similarly, Gracelyn is learning that military leadership is built on a foundation of disciplined followership—understanding your place in the chain of command before you can effectively command others.

The call center eventually became one of the most successful programs at the VA. Not because I had all the right qualifications when I started, but because I was willing to do whatever the mission required, even when it felt overwhelming. I learned to tackle the difficult assignments others might avoid, understanding that willingness to face challenges is what separates those who grow from those who stagnate.

When I heard General Rita Aragon-Watson speak recently about her own journey from an uncertain young officer to a two-star general, her words resonated deeply with my experience in the call center. She emphasized the same truth I'd discovered: that faith provides strength for the journey, that excellence develops through practice rather than natural ability, and that leadership requires both courage and humility.

Her advice to young women—"Do not let anyone put limits on you"—reminded me of those early days when colleagues questioned whether a bedside nurse could manage a complex operation. The only real limits, I learned, were the ones I placed on myself through fear or self-doubt.

Now, as I watch Gracelyn navigate her own leadership challenges at the Academy, I'm reminded that the same God who gave me strength to build something from nothing is giving her strength to become the officer she's meant to be. The path won't always be comfortable, and there will be moments when she feels as unqualified as I did standing in that empty office. But if she remembers that God's strength is made perfect in our weakness, she'll discover what I learned: that feeling unqualified is often the first step toward becoming the leader others need you to be.

Amazing Grace Challenge

Think about a time when you were asked to do something that felt beyond your qualifications. How did that experience change you? Consider sharing this story with a young person in your life who may be facing their own moment of feeling unqualified for a new challenge. Remind them that God's strength is sufficient for whatever He calls us to do, even when we can't see how we'll succeed.

Today I witnessed Grace when:

Finding Strength in
Uncomfortable Moments

*Gracelyn Tramba, Plebe Summer at Naval Academy. Photo
Credit: Thorton Studios, Annapolis, MD.*

*My grace is sufficient for you, for my power is made
perfect in weakness.* —2 Corinthians 12:9 (NIV)

The first few weeks in our retirement community were
filled with moments that made me want to retreat to the
safety of our cottage and close the door. Walking into the
dining room for the first time, scanning for an empty table
while conversations paused and curious eyes assessed the new
residents. Attending my first water aerobics class, I worried I
wouldn't be able to keep up. Sitting in the community room
for activities, surrounded by people who had known each
other for years, while I knew no one.

Each situation felt uncomfortable in its own way—that
awkward space between wanting to belong and feeling like
an outsider. My instinct was to avoid these moments, to eat
meals in our cottage, to skip the group activities, to wait until
I felt more confident before engaging. But together, Norm
and I concluded, "We didn't move here to hide. We moved
here to live."

The very thing I was avoiding—the discomfort of being
new, of not knowing where I fit—was exactly what I needed
to embrace to build the life we'd come here to find.

I think about Gracelyn during those same weeks,
navigating her own uncomfortable moments at the Naval
Academy. Every day brought situations designed to push her
beyond her comfort zone—speaking up in classes where she
might give the wrong answer, leading her company when
she wasn't sure of the direction, and standing for inspection
knowing she might fail to meet standards. Like me, she could
have retreated, could have tried to blend into the background
and avoid the risk of looking foolish.

But both of us were learning the same truth: growth only happens when we're willing to sit in discomfort rather than escape from it.

I remembered something I'd heard from Jet McCoy speaking at Tommy Frank's Four Star Leadership Conference. He'd started his talk by sitting in complete silence, watching as the audience grew increasingly uncomfortable with the quiet. When he finally spoke, he asked how many people were uncomfortable, then said something that stuck with me: "Good. Because learning to deal with being uncomfortable is one of the most important skills you'll ever develop."

Those first weeks taught me he was right. When I forced myself to walk into that dining room despite my anxiety, I discovered that most people were actually eager to welcome newcomers. When I showed up to water aerobics feeling self-conscious, I found a group of women who were more concerned with encouragement than judgment. When I joined conversations where I didn't know the shared history, I realized that my different perspective was often welcomed rather than dismissed.

Jet McCoy said something else that resonated: "Whatever a person is full of will spill out when they're bumped." I found this to be profoundly true. When small frustrations arose—when I couldn't find the dining room or got lost walking back to our cottage—what came out revealed what was really inside me. Was I filled with patience or irritation? Curiosity or judgment? Grace for myself and others, or harsh criticism?

Those uncomfortable moments became mirrors, showing me not just who I was, but who I wanted to become in this new season. They revealed that my character wasn't about how I handled easy days, but how I responded when things felt uncertain or challenging.

Gracelyn was discovering this same truth in her own environment. Every day at the Academy brought tests designed not just to measure knowledge but to reveal character under pressure. How do you respond when you fail an inspection? When you're exhausted but still need to help a struggling classmate? When you're homesick but have duties to fulfill? These weren't just academic challenges—they were character-building opportunities in disguise.

Both of us were learning that discomfort isn't something to be avoided but something to be embraced as a teacher. It shows us where we still need to grow, reveals strength we didn't know we possessed, and builds confidence that can only come from pushing through rather than backing down.

Now, months later, I can walk into any community gathering with genuine confidence—not because I'm no longer capable of feeling uncomfortable, but because I've learned that discomfort is temporary while the growth it produces is lasting. I've discovered that the people I respect most in our community aren't those who never feel uncertain, but those who feel uncertain and show up anyway.

The next time you find yourself in an uncomfortable situation—whether it's joining a new group, having a difficult conversation, or simply trying something you've never done before—remember that this feeling isn't a warning to retreat. It's an invitation to grow. Ask yourself: What is this discomfort trying to teach me? How might I be different on the other side of this challenge?

The answers to these questions, pursued with courage and grace, will shape not just your character but your capacity for joy in whatever new season God has prepared for you.

Amazing Grace Challenge

Identify one situation you've been avoiding because it feels uncomfortable—perhaps joining a group activity, reaching out to someone new, or trying something you've always wanted to do but felt uncertain about. Take one small step toward embracing this discomfort this week, remembering that growth happens in the space between comfort and retreat.

Today I witnessed Grace when:

Vitamin Joy

Zella Leffel and Gracelyn's friendship bring joy.
Photo Credit: Katy Leffel.

A joyful heart is good medicine, but a crushed spirit withers the bones. —Adapted from Proverbs 17:22 (NIV)

Like vitamins that nourish our bodies, joy is an essential nutrient for the soul. Without our daily dose of Vitamin Joy, our spirits begin to wither, but with it, we flourish regardless of our circumstances.

I learned this truth in our old white weathered barn, where Dad taught me that joy often hides in the most ordinary moments. Each evening, I'd watch him balance perfectly on his one-legged milking stool while the barn cats gathered in hopeful circles around Bess, our Jersey cow. With practiced precision, Dad would aim streams of warm milk directly into the kittens' open mouths. Their satisfied purring and my delighted laughter created a symphony of contentment that still echoes in my memory.

Those barn evenings weren't just about chores—they were about discovering that joy doesn't require special occasions or perfect circumstances. It emerges when we're fully present in simple moments, finding wonder in the everyday rhythms of life.

I think of my Christmas colt, naturally named Joy, who taught me that some gifts are living reminders of happiness itself. When Dad took me to the animal auction in Pratt, Kansas, and placed a small brown puppy in my lap, I discovered that joy could be something you hold, something warm and genuine and yours to nurture.

These farm experiences taught me that joy isn't just an emotion—it's a choice we make about how to see our world. Even during difficult seasons, like the harsh Kansas winters or lean financial times, Dad would point out a brilliant sunset or pause to appreciate Mom's fresh bread cooling on the windowsill. He understood that joy is both a gift we receive and a practice we cultivate.

Now I watch Gracelyn learning this same lesson in a vastly different environment. The Naval Academy strips away many of life's familiar comforts—no spontaneous family dinners, leisurely phone calls with friends, no freedom to drive home when homesickness hits. Yet she's discovering joy in unexpected places: the satisfaction of mastering a difficult drill, learning to shoot a pistol, the camaraderie built through shared challenges, the pride in representing something greater than herself.

Her letters reveal moments of pure happiness—celebrating a classmate's success, finding humor during grueling training exercises, or experiencing the thrill of sailing on the Chesapeake Bay. Like those evenings in our barn, her joy emerges not from perfect circumstances but from choosing to notice beauty and meaning within demanding routines.

The Academy is teaching her what our farm taught me: that joy doesn't depend on comfort or convenience. It grows when we're fully engaged in our purpose, when we find connection with others despite difficult circumstances, and when we choose gratitude over complaint.

Here in our retirement community, I've rediscovered this truth in new ways. Shared meals with neighbors replace solitary dinners in front of the television. The freedom to choose how I spend each day feels like an unexpected gift after decades of scheduled obligations. But most importantly, I've learned to savor small moments: a cardinal at the window, Norm bringing me a steaming cup of my favorite coffee, a spontaneous conversation that turns into a lasting friendship.

Both Gracelyn and I are learning that Vitamin Joy isn't about avoiding life's challenges; it's about finding light within them. She finds it in the discipline and purpose of military training; I see it in relationships and the reflection of retirement living. Whether you're twenty and pushing your physical limits at the

Academy or in your golden years with time to truly see and appreciate life's gifts, joy remains available to those who actively seek it.

The difference between happiness and joy is that happiness depends on events, while joy comes from choosing to see God's presence in every circumstance. It's medicine for the soul that we must take daily, intentionally, gratefully knowing that even in our most challenging seasons, there are still barn cats to feed and sunsets to notice.

Amazing Grace Challenge

Create your own joy inventory. Identify three simple, everyday moments that bring you genuine happiness—perhaps morning coffee, a phone call with family, or watching birds at your feeder. These aren't once-in-a-lifetime experiences but ordinary moments available to you regularly. Commit to noticing and savoring these daily doses of Vitamin Joy. Remember, joy isn't optional; it's essential for thriving at any age.

Today I witnessed Grace when:

A Community Where No One Grieves Alone

Combines and trucks stand in formation across a golden wheat field. Photo Credit: Centerview Kansas Co-op.

Bear one another's burdens and so fulfill the law of Christ. —Galatians 6:2 (NIV)

I received a photograph that captured something words alone could never express. Over twenty combines and trucks stood in formation across a golden wheat field, each machine representing more than agricultural equipment—they were instruments of compassion, converging in silent solidarity to support Jay Derley in his most profound moment of vulnerability following the passing of his wife Amy.

The story begins in the 1970s with a simple handshake between two men—Lester Derley and my father, Carl Donovan. More than a business agreement, that handshake became a covenant that would weave through generations. When Lester started farming for Dad, his son Jay eventually continued the legacy, becoming woven into the fabric of our family through shared seasons of planting and harvesting.

When Jay's young wife Amy passed away, he was left with fields ready for harvest and a grief too heavy to bear alone. The farming community's response was swift and complete. At dawn, over twenty combines, twenty-five semi-trucks, and nearly a hundred people descended upon Jay's fields—not as hired workers, but as extended family.

The local co-op coordinated efforts with quiet efficiency while women from three counties arrived with steaming casseroles and fresh-baked pies, setting up makeshift tables at the field's edge. This wasn't just about harvesting wheat—it was about ensuring that in Jay's darkest hour, he would not face his burden alone.

Looking at the names of those who helped that day, I see a tapestry of lifelong relationships: childhood friends, cousins, boys I once babysat, now grown with children of their own.

Each person represents not just a helper, but a connection that time and hardship have only strengthened.

This experience taught me that true community reveals itself not in good times, but in moments when someone can no longer stand alone. These farmers understood something profound: when tragedy strikes one of your own, you pause your own endless work to become the hands and feet of grace.

I think of Gracelyn at the Naval Academy, where she's discovering her own version of this truth. When she received devastating news that her Daddy was having emergency surgery, the chaplain and her midshipmen friends from her company responded with the same instinctive precision as those farmers in Jay's field. In other instances classmates will spend their precious free time tutoring struggling friends, how they'll quietly cover duties for someone facing a family crisis, how they'll stand together in formation not just for inspection but as a wall of support.

The Academy has taught Gracelyn what our farming community taught me: strength isn't measured by how much you can bear alone, but by your willingness to help others bear their load. In both wheat fields and naval quarters, people understand that individual success means nothing if your community fails.

Both environments forge bonds through shared hardship and mutual dependence. Just as those farmers knew that Jay's crisis could one day be their own, Gracelyn's classmates understand that the person struggling beside them in formation might be the one who saves their life at sea. The support isn't just kindness—it's survival.

Here in our retirement community, I've found this same spirit in a gentler form. When a neighbor faces health scares or the loss of a spouse, we gather not with combines but with hugs, not with trucks but with time and presence. We ensure that in life's most difficult seasons, no one walks alone.

Whether it's farmers converging on a grieving man's wheat field, midshipmen rallying around a struggling classmate, or neighbors checking on each other during difficult days, the principle remains constant: we are designed for community, called to bear one another's burdens, and blessed when we answer that call.

The photograph of those combines still moves me because it captures grace in action—love made visible; community transformed from concept to commitment. In a world that often feels fragmented and disconnected, it reminds us that true belonging means showing up when it's hard, staying present when presence is needed, and ensuring that no one—absolutely no one—grieves alone.

Amazing Grace Challenge

Look around your community today. Who might be carrying a burden too heavy for one person to bear? Sometimes the greatest gift we can offer isn't advice or solutions, but simply our presence and practical help. Consider how you might be part of someone's "combines in the field" moment—showing up when it matters most.

Today I witnessed Grace when:

A Different Kind of Christmas Morning

Gifting for the holidays. Photo Credit: Wikimedia Commons.

*Weeping may linger for the night, but joy comes with
the morning.* —Psalm 30:5 (NIV)

During my single years, Christmas mornings arrived with a predictable ache. While families gathered around trees laden with presents, I faced empty rooms and silence that seemed to echo with everything I didn't have. The solution became simple: I volunteered to work every holiday shift at the hospital.

Initially, this wasn't about noble service; it was about survival. Working Christmas Day meant avoiding the painful contrast between my solitary existence and the joyful celebrations happening in homes throughout the city. If I stayed busy caring for patients, I couldn't dwell on my own loneliness or wonder what it would feel like to have someone waiting for me to come home.

But something unexpected happened during those holiday shifts. Walking into the hospital on Christmas morning, I discovered I wasn't alone in seeking refuge in service. Several other nurses and staff members had made similar choices, and together we created our own kind of family among the patients who couldn't go home for the holidays. We shared coffee and homemade cookies that someone had brought from home. We listened to carols playing softly in the hallways. We made sure every patient received attention and felt remembered on a day when being forgotten felt particularly cruel.

What began as an escape from my own pain gradually transformed into a genuine purpose. Instead of feeling sorry for myself, I felt useful. Instead of dwelling on what I lacked, I focused on bringing comfort to people facing their own difficult circumstances. The loneliness didn't disappear—it never completely does—but it transformed into something that could coexist with gratitude and even moments of genuine connection.

Those hospital Christmas mornings taught me that sometimes the best antidote to our own pain is focusing on alleviating someone else's. When isolation threatens to overwhelm, turning outward rather than inward creates space for something meaningful to emerge alongside the sorrow.

Forty years later, the lesson came full circle in the most beautiful way. After marrying Norm and building a life together, we began a new Christmas tradition: inviting people who would otherwise celebrate alone to join us in our home. Single neighbors, widowed friends, anyone who needed a place at the table found one with us. Our dining room was filled with what I came to think of as "chosen family"—a tapestry of people brought together not by blood, but by the understanding that no one should face the holidays alone.

I think of Gracelyn learning her own lessons about finding family in unexpected places. Military service means she may spend many holidays away from home, stationed on ships or at distant bases, creating new kinds of Christmas celebrations with her fellow officers. Like those of us who chose to work holiday shifts or who open our homes to others, she's discovering that meaningful connection can emerge from the most unlikely circumstances.

The Academy is teaching her what I learned during those solitary years and later as a host: sometimes the families we create matter as much as the ones we're born into. Both experiences—working alone on holidays and later hosting others—taught me that love multiplies when shared and that service, whether born from necessity or abundance, has the power to transform both giver and receiver.

Here in our retirement community, I see this same truth unfolding as neighbors reach out to one another during difficult times. We check on those spending their first holidays alone, include them in small gatherings, and create new traditions that honor both our losses and our continued capacity for connection.

The journey from working holidays to avoid loneliness to hosting holidays to prevent others' loneliness wasn't planned, but it was perfect. Those early Christmas mornings at the hospital, born from my own need to escape empty rooms, prepared me to recognize and respond to that same need in others decades later.

The key isn't eliminating sadness from the holidays—that's neither possible nor necessary. It's learning that service, whether motivated by our own pain or our desire to alleviate others', has the power to transform ordinary moments into sacred ones, and lonely hearts into loving communities.

Amazing Grace Challenge

Whether you're facing a difficult holiday season or enjoying one surrounded by loved ones, consider how you might serve others who need connection. Sometimes we serve to heal our own pain; sometimes we serve from a place of abundance to prevent others' pain. Both motivations create the same result: no one has to face holidays alone.

Today I witnessed Grace when:

Nebraska Homecoming: Finding Peace at The Farm

♥

The Farm. Photo Credit: Carolyn Pavlish.

He makes me lie down in green pastures, he
leads me beside quiet waters, he refreshes my soul.
—Psalm 23:2-3 (NIV)

There's something sacred about returning to your roots. For Norm, who spent his first eighteen years in Wilber, Nebraska, last weekend marked another meaningful homecoming as we traveled back to speak at the Saline County Historical Museum. Rather than staying in an anonymous hotel, we chose The Farm, a charming Airbnb nestled just west of Crete, Nebraska.

From the moment our car crunched down the gravel driveway, this place felt like coming home to a story we'd been waiting to hear.

Neal and Carolyn Pavlish welcomed us with the genuine warmth that seems as natural to Nebraska farm country as morning dew on corn silk. Having spent his entire life on this property, Neal doesn't just live here—he's rooted here, part of the soil itself. His stories weren't merely about a place; they were about legacy, about the sacred trust of stewardship passed from one generation to the next.

At The Farm, nature provides a gentler awakening than any alarm clock. I stirred to the persistent mooing of a mother cow searching for her calf—the same adventurous little black one we'd watched the evening before as it squeezed under the fence, driven by that irrepressible curiosity that leads all young creatures to test boundaries.

Nearby, chickens remained safely secured in their coop after a local fox had recently developed an expensive taste for Neal's poultry. As farmers have done for centuries, Neal had adapted his methods to outwit the clever predator—another chapter in the eternal dance between man and nature that defines agricultural life.

The Farm awakened dormant memories that felt as immediate as yesterday's sunset. When barn cats gathered around us, I was transported back decades to my childhood, watching my father milk cows with his distinctive rhythm. I could almost see him again balanced on that one-legged stool, sending perfect streams of warm milk into the eager mouths of waiting kittens. The cats' satisfied purring had provided the soundtrack to countless peaceful evenings in our barn.

What makes The Farm truly special is Neal and Carolyn's commitment to education. They regularly host school groups, creating bridges between city children and the source of their food. Neal's eyes light up as he displays his collection of tractors and antique equipment, allowing children to climb into driver's seats and imagine themselves working the land.

The children's faces transform with wonder as they feed grass to curious cattle through the fence. Neal teaches them that food doesn't simply appear in grocery stores—it emerges from soil tended by hands that understand the responsibility of feeding others. His white corn will eventually journey to Mexico to become tortillas that grace dinner tables across America.

Watching Neal tend his land from dawn to dusk reminded me of Jay Derley, who now farms our family's homestead in Kansas. That evening, I felt compelled to write him, expressing our pride in his stewardship. My father would approve of Jay's careful attention to the soil that supported generations of our family.

Rocky, the faithful farm dog, greeted us at the gate alongside two diligent black-and-white cats who maintained their posts on the front porch. I invited Rocky inside for warmth, but he politely declined, understanding his purpose was to stand sentinel with his feline companions, protecting this peaceful corner of the world.

As Neal worked his land and shared his knowledge about visiting with children, I thought about different kinds of calling.

He's found his purpose in tending the soil and educating the next generation about where their food comes from. Others, like Gracelyn at the Naval Academy, are discovering their calling in service to our country. Whether feeding people or protecting freedoms, some work quietly sustains the world we all depend on.

There's beauty in understanding that each person finds their own way to serve something larger than themselves. The specific calling matters less than the commitment to faithful stewardship—whether of land, family, community, or nation.

If the relentless pace of contemporary life overwhelms you, consider seeking out places like The Farm. There's healing in watching someone care for the land with patience and dedication, in hearing stories that connect us to our roots, in remembering that the most essential work often happens quietly, day after day, season after season.

Amazing Grace Challenge

Consider the "soil" you're tending in your own life—whether it's relationships, community involvement, or caring for others. Take time this week to connect with something that grounds you, whether it's visiting a place from your past, spending time in nature, or simply sitting quietly and remembering what first taught you about belonging. Share one meaningful memory from your childhood with someone you care about.

Today I witnessed Grace when:

A Message from
Grandma Vi

♥

Photo Credit: Wikimedia Commons

If that is how God clothes the grass of the field, which
is here today and tomorrow is thrown into the fire,
how much more will he clothe you—you of little faith!
—Luke 12:28 (NIV)

I never had the chance to meet my grandmother, Viola Susan Summer. She passed away before I reconnected with my birth siblings, but her legacy found its way to me through my sister Sue in Pennsylvania, who lent me Grandma Vi's treasured Bible.

That Bible became an unexpected source of comfort during the uncertain days of 2020. While we were all sheltering during the pandemic, I found myself drawn to its well-worn pages, discovering the handwritten notes that revealed glimpses of Grandma Vi's faith journey.

One passage stopped me in my tracks. Next to Luke 12:26-30, in her careful script, she had written: "This Scripture lesson carried me through the seven years of the Depression and was tough, but we came through it with God's help."

The verses she clung to remind us that if God clothes the grass of the field, how much more will He clothe us. They encourage us not to set our hearts on worry about tomorrow's needs, but to trust in divine provision.

I researched the Great Depression to better understand what Grandma Vi endured. It lasted for seven years, beginning in 1929, and was the longest and most severe economic crisis in modern history—marked by unemployment, bank failures, and widespread poverty. During those difficult years, my great-grandparents, James and Ethel Donovan, nearly lost their farm in Centerview, Kansas. Only through my parents' willingness to take over the financial burden was the family land saved.

What strikes me most is Grandma Vi's perseverance. Seven years of praying through hardship. Seven years of holding onto faith when circumstances seemed impossible. Her steadfast trust puts my own worries into perspective.

Today, having a granddaughter in the Naval Academy, I find myself praying for our troubled world with new urgency. Gracelyn and her fellow midshipmen are preparing to serve in a world facing challenges that would have been unimaginable to Grandma Vi. They will navigate conflicts in Ukraine and the Middle East, address the impacts of climate change, manage technological disruptions, and work toward peace in an increasingly connected yet divided global community.

I pray for wisdom in our leaders—those making decisions today that will shape the world for Gracelyn, our other grandchildren, and their generation to inherit. The choices being made now about international relations, environmental policies, and global cooperation will determine whether our grandchildren serve in a world moving toward peace or one fractured by division.

Sometimes, the weight of global concerns can feel overwhelming. Will there be clean water and breathable air for future generations? Can nations learn to resolve conflicts without warfare? Will democracy and human rights survive the pressures of our time? Will our grandchildren know a world where differences are celebrated rather than feared?

But then, as worry creeps in, I remember a simple childhood song: "He's Got the Whole World in His Hands." In that moment, Grandma Vi's faith becomes my own, and peace settles over my heart once again.

Grandma Vi couldn't have imagined the world we live in today, just as we can't fully envision the world our grandchildren will inhabit. But her example teaches us that faith isn't about having all the answers—it's about trusting in God's provision through uncertain times.

I pray that Gracelyn and her generation will carry forward the best of what we've learned while finding new ways to heal our world's wounds. I pray they'll be peacemakers, bridge-builders, and stewards of creation. Most importantly, I pray they'll remember that even in the darkest times, they are held in loving hands.

When I worry about the complex challenges they'll face—from artificial intelligence to global warming, from economic inequality to international tensions—I try to remember that each generation has faced seemingly insurmountable obstacles. Grandma Vi's generation survived the Depression and World War II. My generation lived through the Cold War and the social upheaval that followed. Our grandchildren will find their own way through whatever trials await them.

The thread that connects us all is faith—faith that love is stronger than hate, that hope overcomes despair, and that God's hands are big enough to hold our troubled world and guide it toward healing.

Amazing Grace Challenge

Today, take time to pray for your family, friends, and the leaders making decisions that affect us all. When worry about the future threatens to overwhelm, remember Grandma Vi's example and give thanks—God truly does hold the whole world in His hands, including the world our grandchildren will inherit.

Today I witnessed Grace when:

Embracing The New Year: Aging with Grace and Hope

♥

Dana writing Grace Goals. Photo Credit: Norm Tramba.

I know the plans I have in mind for you, declares the Lord; they are plans for peace, not a disaster, to give you a future filled with hope. —Jeremiah 29:11 (NIV)

The countdown begins at 11:59, and I'm exactly where I want to be—curled up on our couch beside Norm, watching the glittering ball descend in Times Square from the comfort of our living room. The electric fireplace casts a warm glow, and there's something deeply satisfying about celebrating this moment without the chaos of crowded parties or the obligation to stay out past my bedtime. This isn't settling for less; this is choosing what nourishes my soul.

I think about New Year's Eves from decades past—the pressure to make grand gestures, the exhausting parties, the resolutions that felt more like punishment than promise. Now I understand that growing older isn't about diminishing expectations but about refining them, learning to distinguish between what we think we should want and what actually brings us peace.

As this year closes, I've been practicing a different kind of reflection. Rather than harsh self-criticism about what I didn't accomplish, I'm learning to review my year with the same gentleness I'd show a dear friend. What moments brought unexpected joy? Which challenges revealed hidden strength? There were mornings when I was grateful simply to awake, afternoons when a neighbor's smile changed my entire day, and evenings when Norm and I sat in comfortable silence, our decades together speaking louder than words.

This year, I'm abandoning traditional resolutions in favor of what I call "grace goals," gentle intentions that honor who I'm becoming rather than demanding who I think I should be. Grace goals acknowledge where I am now while inviting growth without judgment. Instead of resolving to exercise more, I'm choosing to move my body with kindness. Instead of promising to be more social, I'm committing to be more present with the people who already enrich my life.

The friends I've found in our retirement community have taught me something remarkable about the value of connection. These are relationships formed not from shared history, but from a shared understanding. We recognize something essential in each other—the wisdom that comes from weathering storms, the humor that emerges from life's absurdities, the tenderness that grows when you realize how precious time truly is.

Tanya Cox and I can sit for hours without running out of stories to share. Norm and her husband, Don, know exactly when we need encouragement and when we need space. These friendships feel both brand new and timeless, as if we were always meant to find each other in this season.

I often think about Gracelyn during these winter weeks at the Naval Academy. While I'm learning the luxury of choice—selecting which activities bring me joy and which relationships deserve my energy—she's discovering the discipline of commitment. Her days are structured by duty rather than desire; her schedule is determined by the demands of leadership training rather than personal preference. Yet in her own way, she's learning grace under pressure, the kind of character that emerges when you can't simply walk away from difficulty.

There's profound beauty in our parallel journeys. She's saying yes to everything asked of her, building the foundation of integrity and service that will define her adult life. I'm learning to say no to anything that doesn't align with who I'm becoming in this season, creating space for deeper joy and authentic connection. Both paths require courage—hers to embrace the unknown challenges ahead, mine to release the expectations that no longer serve me.

My approach to self-care has evolved beyond doctor appointments and prescription schedules, though those remain important. It now means honoring my body's need for gentle movement—water aerobics that make me feel graceful again, morning walks that clear my mind, stretching that reminds me I'm still flexible in more ways than one. Self-care includes feeding my spirit through quiet reflection, journaling thoughts I want to remember, and saying no to commitments that drain more than they give.

Growing older isn't about doing less; it's about making better choices. Our bodies may move more slowly, but our hearts can love more deeply. Our energy may be finite, but our wisdom is expansive. Each day remains a gift, not because we're running out of them, but because we finally understand their true value.

This new year, I'm releasing whatever weighs me down without lifting me up. I'm making room for wonder, for the small miracles that happen when we pay attention, for the grace that appears when we stop demanding and start receiving. Some days will be harder than others, but even on the difficult ones, I know there will be something—a warm cup of tea, a kind word from a neighbor, a memory that makes me smile—that reminds me how blessed this journey has been.

Gracelyn is learning that excellence requires discipline, that leadership demands sacrifice, that grace under pressure builds character. I pray that whatever challenges await her in Annapolis, she'll meet them with the same steady determination that has brought her this far. Her willingness to serve something greater than herself fills me with pride and hope.

As for me, I'm learning that this season of life isn't about winding down but about deepening—into wisdom, into gratitude, into the kind of peace that can only come from accepting exactly where you are. Age doesn't determine worth;

love, accumulated wisdom, and the hope we carry forward
do. We are precisely where we're meant to be, walking a path
illuminated by grace and endless with possibility.

Amazing Grace Challenge

Create your own "Grace Goals" for the new year. Instead of
traditional resolutions that often lead to disappointment, write
down three gentle intentions that honor where you are in life
right now.

Choose one goal for your heart (perhaps deepening a
friendship or practicing daily gratitude), one for your body
(maybe a peaceful morning walk or trying a new gentle activity),
and one for your spirit (such as spending quiet time in reflection
or exploring a creative interest you've always wanted to pursue).

Write these on a beautiful piece of paper and place it
somewhere you'll see it daily—not as pressure, but as gentle
reminders of the grace-filled life you're cultivating.

Today I witnessed Grace when:

Acknowledgements

Carl Donovan — You didn't speak often about God, but you lived your faith in ways that taught me everything I needed to know. I was so blessed to have you as my daddy. God knew exactly who I needed in my life.

Cathy Franks — You sacrificed precious time to read my drafts, offering insights that made every page better. You and Tommy have not only encouraged me to keep writing but have also cheered Gracelyn on to be wonderfully FEISTY. Your friendship is a gift.

Women of Wonder (WOW) — My golden age friends from Touchmark who listened to my stories week after week, you are examples of what it means to live with amazing grace. Thank you for being my first audience and for your constant encouragement.

Tanya Cox — You are so much more than a friend—it feels like having a sister from another mother. Together we've become a little writing gang, spurring each other on to keep putting words on paper.

Boni McBride, Deena Burns, and Shirlee Smith — You are always asking when I'm publishing my next book. Thank you for the constant encouragement and for believing there will always be a "next book" to anticipate.

Nancy Williams — For generously reading my manuscript and, drawing on your experience as a Blue and Gold Officer, providing invaluable insights into Navy life that ensured the authenticity of Gracelyn's Naval Academy experience.

Zella Leffel and Linda Anderson — Zella was Gracelyn's cherished companion throughout the first eighteen years of her life. Through their friendship, we were blessed to welcome Zella's grandmother, Linda, into our retirement community, where a meaningful friendship has flourished in this season of our lives.

General Rita Aragon-Watson and Jet McCoy — I am grateful for your inspiring presentations to the Tommy Franks Leadership students, which provided profound insights that shaped portions of this book. Your leadership examples have been transformational for countless young leaders.

Todd and Somer — Thank you for allowing Gracelyn to chase her dreams with courage and determination. Your belief in her made all the difference.

Troy and Cat — You check on us daily and never stop encouraging us. It's funny how the parenting roles have switched, isn't it? Your love and care mean the world.

Norm — Gracelyn may have the majority of your DNA, but you have 100% of my heart. You take care of everything that needs fixing so I can keep writing. Thank you for being my steady anchor through every season.

Quill Hawk Publishing — To Amy M. Le and the team at Quill Hawk Publishing: I am deeply grateful for the extraordinary care and expertise you brought to this project. In working with you, I witnessed the very essence of what *Amazing Grace* means—thank you for believing in this work and seeing it through with such commitment.

About the Author

Dana Tramba discovered the power of storytelling later in life—and it changed everything. What began as a personal journey to make sense of her own experiences became a passion for helping others uncover the extraordinary within their ordinary moments.

Author of the memoir, *Making Peace with the Pieces of My Life and Living Fully Now.* Dana has spent years collecting life's lessons and turning them into stories that connect generations. She facilitates memoir classes with her curriculum, *"Save Your Life One Story at a Time,"* helping participants discover that every person is the author of their own remarkable story.

Amazing Grace was born from watching her granddaughter, Gracelyn, navigate the Naval Academy while Dana herself learned the challenges of living in a retirement community.

The parallel journeys revealed universal truths about character, faith, and the courage required for any life transition.

Visit Dana at Dandystories.com where she continues to share stories that bridge generations and celebrate the amazing grace found in everyday moments.

www.ingramcontent.com/pod-product-compliance
Lightning Source LLC
Chambersburg PA
CBHW061608120626
46550CB00004B/1648

* 9 7 8 1 9 6 5 1 4 2 6 8 4 *